K. Hoffman

Basic Grammar for Writing

D1306355

Basic Grammar
for Writing

EUGENE EHRLICH

DANIEL MURPHY

McGraw-Hill Book Company

New York   St. Louis   San Francisco   Düsseldorf   Johannesburg
Kuala Lumpur   London   Mexico   Montreal   New Delhi   Panama
Rio de Janeiro   Singapore   Sydney   Toronto

Acknowledgment

Julian Huxley, *Evolution in Action*
Reprinted by permission of Harper & Row, Publishers, Inc.

Basic Grammar for Writing

Copyright © 1967 by Eugene Ehrlich and Daniel Murphy. All rights
reserved. Printed in the United States of America. No part of this
publication may be reproduced, stored in a retrieval system, or
transmitted, in any form or by any means, electronic, mechanical,
photocopying, recording, or otherwise, without the prior written
permission of the publisher.

07-019103-4

890 MU MU 79876

PREFACE

The student who wishes to refresh his memory of grammar can make an excellent start by working systematically through this self-teaching text.

In developing *Basic Grammar for Writing*, we have kept the needs of writers foremost. Our experience over the years with students of composition has shaped our selection of grammatical terms and the exercise materials presented. By concentrating only on those elements of grammar that are most useful for effective writing, this book enables the student to move ahead quickly.

To use this book, begin with the comprehensive review—the initial test—on page 1. Go on to Lesson 1 on the functions of words in simple sentences. Do one new lesson each day. Take all the tests and do all the exercises. By the time you have finished the tenth lesson and the final test following it, you will have reviewed all the essentials of English grammar and will be ready to write effective sentences.

Eugene Ehrlich
Daniel Murphy

CONTENTS

Basic Grammar for Writing

THEME CORRECTION SYMBOLS

agr	mistake in *agreement*
amb	*ambiguous,* open to varying interpretations
awk	*awkward,* clumsy, unnatural, or unpleasant word order
coh	lack of *coherent* relation between sentences
cf	*common fault:* lack of comma, unnecessary comma, or comma insufficient for construction
dangl	*dangling modifier,* unrelated to any sentence element
dead	*deadwood:* unnecessary words
dict	mistake in *diction,* poor choice of words
emph	lacking *emphasis*
fig	inappropriate *figure of speech*
frag	sentence *fragment,* incomplete sentence
HK	*hackneyed,* trite expression
hyph	mistake in *hyphenation,* inappropriate syllabication
mis mod	*misplaced modifier*
no ¶	*no paragraph,* material belongs in previous paragraph
¶	*paragraph:* new paragraph begins here
p	*punctuation* problem
∥	lacking *parallel* construction
ref	*reference:* unclear relationship between pronoun and antecedent
rep	ineffective *repetition* of word or meaning
sp	*spelling error*
stut	*stutter* construction: overuse of verb "to be" (it is, there is, there are)
t	error in *tense*
∿	transpose to correct word order
Ⓦ	*write* out
wdy	*wordiness*
X	carelessness, typing error

INITIAL TEST

Underscore the subject and verb of each **independent** *clause in the following sentences:*

1. Although they had done all they could, the engineers failed to complete the project on time.

2. Scholarly work often leads to practical results, even if the scholars have no thought of practicality when they begin to work.

3. The two brothers decided that there was not enough work to keep them busy.

4. The space initially occupied by the Center is modest by graduate school standards; the total area is twelve thousand square feet.

5. New York City has long been known as the center of education in the United States, but many have criticized New York for its numerous innovations in pedagogy.

6. The novels of Joyce Cary have reached thousands of readers, and his posthumous fame has exceeded that which he enjoyed in his lifetime.

Underscore the subject and verb in each **dependent** *clause of the following sentences:*

7. When they arrived at the beach, the boys quickly stripped to their underwear.

8. John turned out to be an excellent host and showed concern for everyone at the party.

9. The business that was for sale did not suit any of the prospective purchasers.

10. All of us hoped that nothing would be done.

11. I was amazed by his interest, since he had always avoided me in the past.

The italicized modifiers in each of the following sentences relate to a principal sentence element. Write S (subject), V (verb), or O (object) over each modifier to indicate its relationship to one of the sentence elements:

12. *As he walked along the street,* McCann daydreamed.

13. Macbeth, *Shakespeare's only structurally uncomplicated play,* is one *of his shorter tragedies.*

14. William Butler Yeats is *the most widely* admired, *by common reader and sophisticate alike, of all modern poets who have written in English.*

15. He explained *his unusual and complex* product.

16. In 1854, the life of Israel Potter, *an historical writer,* was serialized *in a popular magazine.*

17. *If he abided by the decision,* he would find himself *at a considerable disadvantage.*

Underscore **all verbs** *in the following sentences:*

18. The lackadaisical student plodded through his work dispiritedly and finally dozed.

19. History is studied by those who seek insight into today's political problems.

20. When built, the Center will be operated by the United States Public Health Service and will study a broad range of environmental health problems.

21. The educational gap between the average rural child in America entering school and the average urban child is enormous, educators are saying aloud for the first time.

22. He said hello and almost smiled.

23. We began to chat in a friendly manner, and he said that these people had to be taught how to live, how to clean house, and how to look after children.

Fill in the blanks in the following sentences with the appropriate forms of the verbs:

24. After the evening newspapers appeared, I (look) for the review of the play that (open) last night.

25. I looked to see whether he (joke)

26. Each morning, as the sun (rise) , the milkman (set) out on his rounds.

27. Before the ship had left, they (deliver) the flowers.

28. The most important fact the police know about him is that he (work) in the bank for ten years.

29. The longest home run ever hit in Yankee Stadium
(hit)   by Babe Ruth.

Underscore all errors in **agreement** *and* **reference** *in the following sentences:*

30. The form of your bibliography and footnotes are not standard.

31. A novel or a biography are equally acceptable as the subject of the paper.

32. Modern research concentrates on those types of disease that affects the greatest number of people.

33. This group of essays is concerned with the problems of American democracy.

34. The text of *Moby-Dick* with editorial notes make a fine addition to his personal collection.

35. The tweed jacket, bought long ago from one of London's best tailors, serves as his sports jacket even today.

36. J. Dover Wilson, one of the few Shakespearean critics who senses the importance of the passage, realizes that a large part of the Elizabethan audience would have followed the technicalities of the duel in *Hamlet* as intently as a modern audience follows a poker game in the movies.

Supply fourteen marks of punctuation in the following:

37.-50. Intelligence and creativity are not identical but intelligence does play a role in scientific creativity a role greater than it plays in some other forms of creativity. One may summarize by saying that the minimum intelligence required for creative production in science is considerably better than average but that given this other variables contribute more to variance in performance. It must also be noted that special abilities numerical spatial verbal and so on play somewhat different roles in different scientific fields but that ability must in no case be below average. A cultural anthropologist for example has little need for great facility with numbers. An experimental physicist on the other hand does require facility with numbers although he need not have great facility with words.

For answers, see page 96.

LESSON 1

The Sentence: I

A simple English sentence is composed of a *subject* and a *verb* – and sometimes an *object*.

In the sentence

The cat chased the rat.

cat is the subject, *chased* is the verb, and *rat* is the object.

Why do we say this? An action is being performed in the sentence. It is concerned with "chasing."

If we ask who or what is performing the action, the answer is *cat* – the subject.

If we ask what the action is, the answer is *chased* – the verb.

If we ask who or what is being chased – the answer is *rat* – the object.

In the simple sentence we have used – and in most English sentences – *subject precedes verb*, and *object follows verb*. This arrangement of sentence elements underlies English grammar and sentence structure. Subject (S) precedes verb (V) – object (O) follows verb (V).

What happens when we manipulate the elements in the sentence?

      S   **V**   **O**
The cat chased the rat.

      S   **V**   **O**
The rat chased the cat.

The individual words have not been changed in any way. Only the order has been changed. Yet the meaning of the second sentence is quite different from that of the first.

There is one special kind of object – the *indirect* (IO). We identify the indirect object by asking whether a sentence contains a secondary sentence element that is related to the object of the verb but does not describe it. Examine the following sentences:

            IO
He gave *the cat* its food.

                  IO
He gave the food *to the cat*.

The direct object in both sentences is *food*. We know this because it answers the question "What is given?"

The indirect object in both sentences is *cat*. We know this because *cat* receives the direct object *food*.

Whenever a sentence element receives a direct object, we call that element the indirect object.

Notice that in the two sentences above, the indirect object occurs in two forms: when it precedes the object, the word *to* is omitted; when it follows the object, a word such as *to* or *for* is needed.

Here are three examples of each sentence form:

Send the *man* a *basket* of flowers.

Send a *basket* of flowers to the *man*.

The physician gave his *patient* the *medicine*.
The physician gave the *medicine* to the *patient*.

She gave *him* a *party* .
She gave a *party* for *him*.

Because of the importance of word order in a sentence, it is worthwhile to examine a few more pairs of sentences that illustrate how changes in word order affect meaning:

Night follows day.
Day follows night.

Nothing is worse than stupidity.
Stupidity is worse than nothing.

The tractor leveled the wall.
The wall leveled the tractor.

Cowardice breeds heroism.
Heroism breeds cowardice.

The bull threw the cowboy.
The cowboy threw the bull.

The verb is the pivot of the sentence, with the subject before it and the object after it. Changing this sequence distorts the meaning of a sentence or, at the least, results in strange-sounding constructions.

Until now, we have been using *simple* (single) subjects, verbs, and objects. Many sentences contain *compound* (two or more) subjects, verbs, and objects. For example:

The boy and girl went up the hill. (compound subject)
The boy ran and skipped all the way home. (compound verb)
The boy carried a ball and bat. (compound object)

Of course, sentences occur that have more than one compound element:

Dictionaries and handbooks were printed and distributed by the publisher.
The student and his brother wrote book reports and term papers.

A series—a structure of more than two units—is also common:

The left fielder, center fielder, and right fielder all played errorless ball.
The dog harassed, attacked, and finally killed the fox.
Milton wrote poetry, prose, and drama.

In certain sentences, such as those that do not make statements but ask questions, the normal order of sentence elements may be reversed.

In the sentence "Where is New York?" the word *where* occupies the subject position but is not the subject. The subject is *New York*.

In the sentence "Is John home?" the verb *is* occupies the subject position but is obviously not the subject.

Other constructions violate the normal subject-verb-object sequence. One such sentence is "There are seven boys in the room." According to any logical grammatical analysis, the verb *are*, being plural, agrees with *boys*, even though *there* is in the subject position. This makes *boys* the subject of *are*.

Even though one of the primary rules of sentence structure is that *verb must agree with subject* (that is, when a subject is plural, the verb must also be plural; when a subject is singular, the verb must also be singular), treating *there* as the subject and calling the construction idiomatic does no harm. No one whose native language is English has any difficulty with this construction. He has only to remember that in *there is* and *there are* sentences the verb must agree with the logical subject.

Certain English sentences do not appear to contain all the main sentence elements. Such sentences as "Run!" and "Stop!" have no subject. "Caution!" has neither subject nor verb. The writer intends that the reader supply the appropriate missing elements:

(you) Run!
(you) Stop!
(you use) Caution!

Certain nonsentences, such as words that express emotional states, have no structure and need no analysis:

Ah.
Gosh.
Horrors!

We capitalize them when they stand alone and we punctuate them as though they were sentences. Yet they are not sentences.

We have spoken thus far of *sentences, subjects, verbs, objects, indirect objects, the order of sentence elements, compounds, series, there is* and *there are, agreement of subject and verb, sentences that do not contain all sentence elements,* and *nonsentences.* The exercises that follow give practice in understanding simple sentence construction. The answers for the exercises begin on page 98. Do the exercises without looking ahead; when you have finished, check them against the correct answers.

If you want to read through this chapter once more before doing the exercise, go right ahead. You are going to be asked to identify *subjects, verbs, objects,* and *indirect objects.* The subject in a sentence tells *who* or *what* is performing the action of the sentence. The verb is the *action.* The object *receives* the action. The indirect object *receives* the object.

REVIEW EXERCISES

In each of the following sentences, place the letter

   S *above subject,*
   V *above verb,*
   O *above object (if one exists),*
   IO *above indirect object (if one exists).*

1. The fat girl ate the food.

2. Newspaper reporters and editors clarify the news.

3. The lake shone and sparkled.

4. The call came last night.

5. Last night he called his mother, sister, and brother.

6. The veterinarian gave the horse an examination.

7. The cat mothered her kittens.

8. Frogs make pleasant sounds.

9. Honey attracts bees.

10. Nothing remained.

11. Why is he in the kitchen?

12. Where are the cake and ice cream?

13. They sent seven boys seven books.

14. There were seven boys in the stream.

15. Stop the bus!

16. The driver stopped the bus.

17. The long-winded orator wound his way through the tortured sentence.

18. Books entertain.

19. Running through the room, the boy stubbed his toe.

20. Nothing is left to do.

The Sentence: II

Complicated thoughts may be expressed in simple sentences, but we then run the risk of writing in primer style—every concept in a simple sentence. In order to avoid monotony and lack of emphasis, more complicated sentence structures must be used. These sentences give us an opportunity to show the relationships and relative importance of the ideas we wish to express.

These more complicated sentences are in three main categories:

- compound
- complex
- compound-complex

COMPOUND SENTENCES

A compound sentence is composed of two or more *independent clauses.* An independent clause is a group of words that must contain a subject and a verb and may contain an object. It is called *independent* because it can stand as a separate sentence. There are three ways to set up a compound sentence.

1. The most frequently used method of joining two independent clauses employs a comma and one of the common connecting words—and, but, or, nor, for, so, yet. Two sentences using these common connecting words will serve as examples:

> The original meanings of many words are lost, but we continue to find new meanings for them.

> He wanted to find his lost book, so he searched all day.

2. Another method is to use a semicolon. When a semicolon is used, no connecting word is necessary.

3. However, style is frequently improved by the use of a connecting word. Sentence A illustrates the use of the semicolon without a connecting word; sentence B illustrates this use of the semicolon with a connecting word.

A. The children asked the question; the teacher supplied the answer.

B. The children asked the question; however, the teacher could not supply the answer.

Each independent clause contains all the necessary sentence elements of a simple sentence. We could have written each clause as a simple sentence.

COMPLEX SENTENCES

A complex sentence is composed of one *independent clause* and one or more *dependent clauses.* A dependent clause contains a subject and verb and may contain an object, but a dependent clause cannot stand as a sentence:

A. The $\overset{s_1}{\text{children}}$ [$\overset{s_2}{\text{who}}$ $\overset{v_2}{\text{asked}}$ the $\overset{o_2}{\text{question}}$] $\overset{v_1}{\text{found}}$ the $\overset{o_1}{\text{answer.}}$

B. The $\overset{s_1}{\text{chair}}$ [$\overset{s_2}{\text{that}}$ $\overset{v_2}{\text{I admired}}$] $\overset{v_1}{\text{was}}$ already $\overset{v_2}{\text{sold.}}$

C. [$\overset{}{\text{Because}}$ the $\overset{s_2}{\text{apples}}$ $\overset{v_2}{\text{were}}$ $\overset{o_2}{\text{inexpensive,}}$] the $\overset{s_1}{\text{housewife}}$ $\overset{v_1}{\text{bought}}$ $\overset{o_1}{\text{them.}}$

D. $\overset{s_1}{\text{He}}$ $\overset{v_1}{\text{hoped}}$ [that the $\overset{s_2}{\text{game}}$ would $\overset{v_2}{\text{end}}$ shortly].

Sentence A contains a dependent clause used as the modifier of the subject. (Modifiers are discussed in Lessons 3 and 4.) The *who* of the dependent clause has two functions. It indicates that a dependent clause is at hand. It also acts as the subject of the dependent clause. This sentence could have been written as two sentences:

The children asked the question. They found the answer.

This is primer style. The reader has no way of knowing which of these two statements is the more important; therefore, one must be subordinated. Obviously the subordination could have been reversed:

> The children who found the answer asked the question.

No matter how the thought is expressed, subordination is required. Sentence B has the same structure as A.

The dependent clause of sentence C is out of its normal order—main statement following subordinate statement. *Because* followed by a subject and verb indicates that a dependent clause is to occur. Even if the clause occurred in its normal position—after the main clause—the use of *because* would indicate that a dependent clause followed.

> The housewife bought the apples because they were inexpensive.

In sentence D, "He hoped that the game would end shortly," the main clause is *he hoped.* The remainder of the sentence functions as the object of the verb. We can determine that the dependent clause is the object of the verb by asking the question "hoped what?" This structure is common in English. (The next two lessons discuss the functions of dependent clauses.)

COMPOUND-COMPLEX SENTENCES

Compound-complex sentences are a combination of the two forms already discussed. One of the two or more independent clauses contains one or more dependent clauses. In the following examples, dependent clauses have been placed in brackets.

> A. This is fair enough for a person [who is acting as an individual], but anyone [who is going to express his opinions in writing for others to read] has a responsibility to examine them closely.
>
> B. [Although he was no longer interested in pursuing the

problem], he persisted in the effort, and his teacher had to relieve him of responsibility for the project.

C. It was the primitive hero [that I had discovered in myself] [that helped me to face the idea of the journey], for there is nothing [that wearies me so much as a long journey in the train].

You can see that complicated concepts cannot be expressed effectively in simple sentences alone. Nor can a writer rely exclusively on complicated structures. Lesson 9 discusses matters of style, and Lesson 10 gives many examples of good and bad writing.

REVIEW EXERCISES

Place brackets around all **dependent** *clauses in the following twenty sentences and identify the* **subject, verb,** *and* **object** *of all clauses. The answers to the first ten sentences are on page 99.*

<pre>
               S   V   O   S
    Example: An astronaut undertakes a rigorous program [that
         V   O
    prepares him for the ardors of space travel].
</pre>

1. I work harder in one day than most people work all week.

2. If I had not lost my car keys, I would have driven to work.

3. Although this was my first speech, I was not nervous at all.

4. Because this tree was the finest example of its type in the county, agricultural agents, from far and wide, came to see it.

5. Some writers follow all the conventions of standard English; others seem to do all they can to avoid this practice.

6. Students who are not prepared for complicated questions usually get poor grades.

7. Some chairs that have arms and backrests are comfortable; others, lacking them, are also comfortable.

8. Successful businessmen show concern for the welfare of their employees, and there is little doubt that they owe much of their success to this concern.

9. Schoolteachers who never permit colloquial expressions in their students' writing might be considered old-fashioned; however, laxness in writing by students who feel that they can get away with anything cannot be admired.

10. Quotation marks are used for titles of written works shorter than volume length, for single poems, short stories, and magazine articles.

11. The landlord said that he would cut off the heat by the end of the month.

12. In spite of all our protests and demonstrations, the mayor, whom the people elected in a landslide, showed his true nature and did nothing.

13. True national spirit depends on unity of purpose, but misguided efforts at unifying the people lead ultimately to disunity.

14. When a student discovers that education requires full-time attention, he has no choice but to apply himself or get out.

15. When the national leadership fails to respond to the will of the people, the electorate must oust that leadership and elect new representatives who will.

16. Poor housing and decaying neighborhoods contribute to weakening morale that ends in despair; the remedy for this is not

wholesale destruction of the neighborhood, but massive programs for rapid improvement.

17. Music that reflects the current mood of people is more likely to be appreciated than music we all recognize as stemming from an earlier age.

18. Clothing worn by young people today strangely resembles that worn by the members of the aristocracy in Europe during the Eighteenth Century, despite the fact that today's youth reject that earlier society.

19. Blacks and Puerto Ricans, who are becoming a more significant part of the leadership group in America, insist that the younger generation enroll in colleges and acquire advanced degrees.

20. Ethnic groups, who are forced to batter their way into the middle class, may find that one of their biggest obstacles is the need to master the English of Middle-America.

LESSON 3

Modifiers: I

Everything in a sentence that is not a subject, verb, object, or indirect object is a *modifier*. A modifier clarifies, limits, or describes the subject, verb, object, or indirect object in a sentence.

Modifiers may consist of single words or groups of words.

ONE-WORD MODIFIERS

Consider the following sentences:

> A. Rainy days sometimes dampen youthful spirits.

The subject, verb, and object—the main sentence elements—are *days dampen spirits*. The modifiers *rainy, sometimes, youthful* limit the main sentence elements. Only *rainy* days, only *sometimes* dampen, only *youthful* spirits.

> B. Many American anthropologists have fully studied primitive societies.

The main sentence elements are *anthropologists have studied societies*. The modifiers *Many American, fully, primitive* limit and clarify these elements. Not all anthropologists, but *Many American;* have *fully* studied; not all societies, but *primitive* societies.

In both sentence, omission of the modifiers would have resulted in entirely different meanings:

> Days dampen spirits.
> Anthropologists have studied societies.

The modifiers in certain sentences do not affect meaning. These modifiers often can be omitted.

Consider the following sentences:

    C. Gracious Eleanor Roosevelt was charitable.

    D. The sturdy oak bears acorns.

Gracious and *sturdy* describe the subjects of the sentences. Clearly we do not need either modifier. Since they add nothing to the sentences, they should be omitted.

Consider the following sentences:

    E. The red convertible sped away.

(When discussing *classes* of words, traditional grammarians identify *the, a* and *an* as articles. It is clear that they are modifiers. Because students have no difficulty with articles, they will not be discussed further in this book.)

This sentence contains two other modifiers. The first one, *red,* limits *convertible.* If the word *automobile* were in the sentence— "the red convertible automobile sped away"—*convertible* would itself be a modifier, limiting *automobile.* Words can perform different functions within a sentence.

Away modifies *sped.* It tells the reader the direction in which the car sped. *Away* answers the question, sped where? In general, modifiers of verbs can be identified by asking of the verb the questions:

    when? where? why? how? or *how much?*

    F. Souvenir statues, hurriedly manufactured, sold briskly everywhere.

Souvenir limits the subject *statues. Manufactured* describes *statues* —they were not chiseled or carved. *Hurriedly* describes *manufactured,* telling us the manner in which manufacture took place. *Hurriedly manufactured* could have been placed before *souvenir;* for emphasis it follows *statues. Briskly* and *everywhere* modify the verb *sold*—they answer the questions *how?* and *where?*

    G. Today, most modern furniture has straight lines.

Modern limits the subject *furniture. Most* modifies *modern furniture,* if we consider both words as a unit. The sentence does not imply *most modern* in the sense of a superlative—modern, more modern, most modern. Nor does *most* modify furniture alone. In fact, most furniture does not have straight lines! *Straight* modifies *lines.* What about *today?* It is closest to *most modern furniture,* which it clearly does not modify. It is also NOT a main sentence element—subject, verb, or object. Whenever you find a word whose function in a sentence is not immediately apparent, ask of the verb the questions, *when? where? why? how?* or *how much?* Generally this procedure will solve the problem. In this case, *today* answers the question "when?"

REVIEW EXERCISES

In each of the following sentences, find and identify the **subject, verb, object,** *and* **indirect object,** *if one exists. Write* S *over subject,* V *over verb,* O *over object, and* IO *over indirect object. Then mark over each modifier the sentence element it modifies (*MS—*modifies subject;* MV—*modifies verb;* MO—*modifies object;* MIO—*modifies indirect object). The answers to the first ten sentences are on page 100.*

          MS   S   MV   V   MO   O

Sample: Soggy doughnuts frequently cause upset stomachs.

1. Generally, old houses give their owners much trouble.

2. The long-winded orator wound his way through the tortuous speech.

3. Running through the room, the boy stubbed his toe.

4. Many physicians now caution their patients against smoking.

5. Apple trees blossom vigorously in the spring.

6. Defeated in battle, the army retreated to the fort.

7. Little can be done after a show has closed.

8. The sea and the wind buffeted the struggling ship, which was far off course.

9. The boy tried hard and finally mastered the difficult subject.

10. Far off to his left, the gladiator saw lions and other beasts coming at him.

11. Crime in the streets certainly must be considered in any plan of municipal reform.

12. A suitable sports arena provides necessary facilities for recreation.

13. Good food and drink have been one of man's most cherished traditions.

14. Adequate social services and moderate taxation make this area one of the most desired in the metropolitan region.

15. The question of adequate water supply plagues many heavily populated states.

16. If we are to maintain current living standards, we must consider the availability of industries capable of producing jobs.

17. Medical care for the aged provides a measure of security for those who need it most.

18. Some cities are so large that they dwarf the smallest states in total population.

19. Can teachers trained twenty years ago meet today's demands in the classroom?

20. Proper legal assistance, even for those who cannot afford it, assures fair treatment for all citizens.

LESSON 4
Modifiers: II

In the preceding chapter, the term *modifier* was defined as any word in a sentence that clarifies, limits, or describes the main sentence elements. *Modifiers* may be more than one word long. Examine the following sentences. What functions do the *italicized groups of words* perform?

> A. *To help his team to victory,* the centerfielder stayed *in the game.*
> B. *Defeated at last,* the team walked *off the field.*
> C. The man *who knows the truth* succeeds.
> D. The repairman found the pole *that had been felled.*
> E. *If we agree,* we can take action.

Each *italicized* group of words *modifies* one of the three main elements of the sentence in which it is found. Note that these groups of words are irreducible—taking any word from the modifier either distorts the meaning or wrecks it completely. Let us examine each of these examples in turn and determine the function of the modifiers.

A. *"To help his team to victory,* the centerfielder stayed *in the game." To help his team to victory* modifies *stayed,* the verb, answering the question "why?" The verb is also modified by *in the game,* which answers the question "where?"

B. *"Defeated at last,* the team walked *off the field." Defeated at last* modifies *team,* the subject, telling the condition of the team. The verb *walked* is modified by *off the field,* answering the question "where?"

All the modifiers in these two sentences are phrases—groups of words without subjects or verbs. In the following sentences, all the modifiers are clauses—groups of words containing a subject and verb.

C. "The man *who knows the truth* succeeds." The subject *man* is modified by *who knows the truth.* This modifier identifies the particular man under discussion.

D. "The repairman found the pole *that had been felled."* The object *pole* is modified by *that had been felled,* identifying a particular pole.

E. "*If we agree,* we can take action." The verb *can take* is modified by *If we agree.* Only if "we" agree, can action take place.

In the discussion up to this point, the examples used have been carefully selected to illustrate single-word and multiple-word modifiers. In typical sentences, modifiers are normally more complex. Single words, phrases, and clauses frequently occur together as modifiers. The following sentence serves to illustrate this complexity:

> In 1794, disheartened, despondent, and embittered against his former friends for their sympathy with the revolution, Burke withdrew his support from his party after nearly thirty years of distinguished service.

In order to find the modifiers in a sentence such as this, a good procedure is to find the main verb or verbs. In this sentence it is *withdrew.* Who or what withdrew? The answer is the subject— *Burke.* Is there an object of the verb? Ask the question, withdrew what? Answer—*support.* We now have identified the main statement —*Burke withdrew support.* We are ready to identify the modifiers. The best way to proceed is to ask of the verb *when? where? why? how?* and *how much?*

When? *In 1794 . . . after nearly thirty years of distinguished service.* Where? *from his party.* The other questions do not apply in this case.

We proceed to the subject. Is the subject described or limited in any way? In this sentence, what has the writer told us about Burke when he withdrew? *disheartened, despondent, and embittered against his former friends for their sympathy with revolution.*

Is the object described or limited in any way? In this case, the word *his* is the sole modifier of the object.

Now it is time to explore the additional complexities within the modifiers already isolated. As we have learned, modifiers may be single words, phrases, or clauses. Single words are always easy to identify. Phrases and clauses may not be. We recall that a phrase is a group of words that does not contain a subject and verb, while a clause does.

First let us examine the modifiers of the subject. *Embittered,* unlike *disheartened* and *despondent,* is itself modified. It is first modified by the phrase *against his former friends.* Why? *for their sympathy.* Surely no one should be despondent over sympathy! It is obvious that some modification of sympathy must be added. When we read *sympathy with revolution,* we have the meaning the writer intended. Thus, by successive limitation, the author has clearly stated his concept.

Turning our attention next to the modifiers of the verb, the only complexity we find is *after nearly thirty years of distinguished service.* There are two phrases coupled within this modifier. The word *years* in the phrase *after nearly thirty years* is a general term that is further clarified by the modifier *of distinguished service.*

The following paragraph includes single-word and multiple-word modifiers. As you read, identify the main elements by S V O IO. Use S_1, V_2, O_3, for example if a sentence has multiple main-sentence elements. Then place brackets around each modifying unit. Above each of these units, write SM (subject modifier), VM (verb modifier), OM (object modifier), or IOM (indirect object modifier) to identify the modifier's function. The answer is on the next page.

The Clearwater and the Garvan Collections are on permanent exhibition in the Metropolitan Museum of New York and together provide a liberal education to the student and collector of early American silverware. Every article in both collections was made in the workshop of a master craftsman. On the death of the original owner, the piece became an heirloom and was handed down, a cherished possession,

from generation to generation, until it passed into the hands

of dealers and auctioneers.

ANSWER

      SM   **S**   **V₁**

[The Clearwater and Garvan] Collections are [on permanent

         V₁M   **V₂M**

exhibition in the Metropolitan Museum of New York] and [togeth-

 V₂   **OM**   **O**   **IO**

er] provide [a liberal] education [to the student and collector] [of

  IOM   **SM**   **S**   **SM**

early American silverware]. [Every] article [in both collections]

V   **VM**   **V₁M**

was made [in the workshop of a master craftsman]. [On the death

                   S   **V**   **O**   **V₂**

of the original owner], the piece became an heirloom and was

    V₂M   **OM**   **V₂M**

handed [down], [a cherished possession], [from generation to

                        V₂M

generation], [until it passed into the hands of dealers and

auctioneers].

Some of the modifiers in this paragraph, such as *Clearwater and Garvan,* need no further discussion. Others, less obvious, require explanation.

The first sentence contains a compound verb, *are* and *provide.* If you can see this, the structure of the modifiers should be clear. In the second sentence, the verb is modified by a long phrase, *in the workshop* .... You can see how each modifier acts on the verb, the first telling *where* every article was made, the other telling *how* it was made. The last sentence has a compound verb, *became* and *was handed,* and a long clause modifying *was handed.* The clause beginning with *until,* has *it* as subject and *passed* as verb. There is no object. The subject is not modified, while the verb is modified by everything else in the clause.

REVIEW EXERCISES

The following paragraphs include single-word and multiple-word modifiers. As you read, identify S, V, O, IO; identify **single-word** modifiers *by* MS, MV, *or* MO; *bracket* **multiple-word modifiers** *and identify in the same manner.*

Correct diction is the basic element in all writing. Words have to be well chosen, for precision increases clarity and interest. Good diction means the absence of ambiguity, obscurity, and misunderstanding.

General words, unlike some scientific ones, have more than one meaning and more than one quality. Most words do not simply *denote* (the meaning found in the dictionary); they also connote— they *imply* meanings in addition to the denoted meaning. Many words have similar denotations, but different connotations; for example, we have many words meaning dog. Consider these: canine, cur, mongrel, and mutt. It is quite obvious that *mutt,* although it means a kind of dog, connotes much more to the reader than simply a dog of undetermined lineage. *Canine* is much more formal and also much less visual than *mutt*—it is less connotative. The situation in which we would choose one of these words for *dog* would be determined by the degree of formality in a paper. Words have different degrees of appropriateness to different writing situations. Writers who wish to use words precisely have the responsibility of considering all aspects of a word.

In addition to all his problems of style, the good writer must pay careful attention to denotation and connotation as he works. Good writing demands this careful attention.

For answers, see page 101.

LESSON 5
Verbs

Verbs

- state the action performed by the subject ,
- classify the subject,
- describe its condition, or
- link the subject with the word performing the object function.

For the purpose of understanding grammar and writing correctly, the type of verb you deal with does not matter. The distinction between *transitive* verbs—those that take objects—*intransitive* verbs—those that do not take objects—and *linking* verbs—those that take complements rather than objects—has no functional importance and will not be considered here.*

Consider these three sentences:
  He *hit* the ball.
  He *stayed* home.
  He *is* handsome

In the first sentence, the verb states the *action* of the subject upon the object. In the second, the verb has no object. *Home* is a modifier—it answers the question "stayed where?" In the third sentence, the verb links the subject with a functional object—*handsome.*

*The word completing the sense of a linking verb is called a *complement.* A linking verb thus serves only to link a subject with a complement. Many students find difficulty in choosing the form of a pronoun after the linking verb *to be.* Formal English calls for the pronoun to be in the *subjective* case: It is I. Informal English most often uses the *objective* case: It is me. (Lesson 7 discusses the forms of pronouns.)

In each sentence, the main elements are in normal order: *subject, verb, object; subject, verb;* and *subject, verb, object, complement.* The problem of identifying the main verb in a sentence is solved by asking: "What is the main statement of the sentence?" In the main statement, the verb will be the word or words that *state* the action or *link* the subject with the words that classify or describe it. Consider these sentences:

> Doctors *examine* patients. (*Examine* is the action in which doctors engage.)
>
> He *solved* the problem. (While the action of *solved* is mental rather than physical, action nevertheless has taken place. *Solved* is the verb.)
>
> He *is* handsome. (The verb *is* links the subject with the word that describes him.)
>
> She *feels* ill. (The verb *feels* links the subject with a word that describes her condition. She feels how?)
>
> Some plays *last* more than three hours. (*Last* describes an aspect of the subject. *Last* is the verb.)

In all the examples cited thus far, the verbs are easy to identify. In many sentences, identifying the verb is more difficult.

Identify the main verbs in these sentences:

> 1. State and city colleges and universities are generally inexpensive for local residents.
> 2. The surest way to be able to pay for college is to put the money aside little by little over the years.
> 3. Success depends on getting started early and keeping work foremost in your life.
> 4. Many physical therapists recommend breathing exercises to increase lung capacity and decrease the work of breathing.

Were you able to identify the main verbs in these four sentences? In the first, the main statement is *colleges and universities are inexpensive,* even though we would not realistically accept this statement without qualification. The verb *are* links the subject with the word that describes it. (Reducing a sentence to its main elements enables you to determine the function of each word.

Remember that all words other than the main sentence elements are modifiers.)

In the second sentence, the main statement is *way is to put*. This conclusion is reached by a difficult process. To follow the reasoning, you will have to call on all the information you have already mastered. *Way* is the subject of *is* (who or what *is?* way *is*). We ask "What *is* the way?" The answer is *to put*. Thus, *is* links *way* and *to put*. Remembering that all words except those in the main statement are modifiers, it becomes obvious that *way* is modified by *surest*. *To be able to pay for college* also modifies *way*. Similarly, the words following *to put* clearly modify it.

The third sentence has *success depends* as its main statement. In this case, everything that follows *depends* qualifies—that is, modifies —it.

The main statement of the fourth sentence is *therapists recommend exercises*. *Recommend* conveys the action of the subject, and all words other than the main statement are modifiers of *therapists* or *exercises*.

As you learned earlier, some main statements contain more than one main verb. Examine the following sentences:

1. Despite the importance of education, some students fight and complain all the way through school.
2. The population of Europe sought and found a way to ease the problem of food shortages.
3. All the residents of the community turned out for the meeting and voiced their complaints.

In each of these sentences, there is more than one main verb: *fight* and *complain; sought* and *found; turned* and *voiced*.

REVIEW EXERCISES

Underscore all **verbs** *in the following sentences. Place check marks over the* **main verbs** *—the verbs in the main statements. Answers to the first ten sentences are on page 102.*

1. Allen Tate was born in Kentucky and was graduated from Vanderbilt University.

2. That is no country for old men.

3. They sat together at a table that was close against the wall near the door of the cafe and looked at the terrace where the tables were all empty except where the old man sat in the shadows of the leaves of the tree that moved slightly in the wind.

4. Using quotation marks to call attention to an ironic or humorous passage is like poking someone in the ribs when you have reached the point of a joke.

5. Since the days of the early Greeks, men have been trying to explain various natural phenomena and find the laws governing them.

6. The Declaration, then, makes sense, and excellent sense.

7. It has been said that if a person were to take a cup of water to the Pacific Ocean, pour it in, and then stir the ocean thoroughly, he would have eight or ten of the original molecules in the cup if he filled it again with ocean water.

8. A man may take to drink because he feels himself a failure, and then fail all the more because he drinks.

9. Modern English is full of bad habits which spread by

imitation and which can be avoided if one is willing to take the necessary trouble.

10. The texts are concerned with political ideas.

11. Children who are forced to grow up in the slums find themselves at a disadvantage when they enter the job market.

12. Dope pushers, who exploit the addict, cannot survive without active assistance of those members of the police force who can be bribed.

13. Addicts commit most of the crimes in the major cities; to curb crime, curb the addict.

14. The difference between those who succeed and those who fail is a question of education.

15. Correction of existing faults is the first step toward improvement of our lives.

16. The Congress has the responsibility of revealing the extent of information-gathering activities of the Federal government.

17. There can be no question that the context of a piece of writing can affect the style in which it is written.

18. Long distance truck drivers are extremely well paid and frequently own the trucks they drive.

19. Malcolm X, who was assassinated years ago, did a great deal for the advancement of the Blacks.

20. The Pentagon spends the major portion of the nation's wealth, which, in view of the plight of the underprivileged, makes little or no sense.

LESSON 6

Verb Tense and Voice

TENSE

Verbs not only state an action or condition of the subject, but they also indicate *when* that action or condition occurred. The time may be present, past, or future. The aspect of a verb that tells us *when* the action occurred is called *tense*. For a discussion of how the tenses of a verb are formed, see the chart on pages 34-35.

Present Tense

The present is the most familiar and most frequently used tense. The following sentences illustrate uses of present tense to describe (A) present conditions or actions, (B) habitual actions, (C) future, and (D) conditions true for all time:

> A. I *feel* well. (present condition) This novel accurately *represents* Victorian society. (present action)
> B. John *walks* to work every day. (habitual action)
> C. Ships *depart* for Europe next week. (simple future)
> D. Doctors *serve* mankind. (true for all time)

We do not often think of these varied uses for the present tense, yet we all employ them in our normal speech and writing.

Past Tenses

The past tenses are *past, present perfect,* and *past perfect.*

PAST

Past describes an action or condition begun and completed in the past:

The author *lived* in the society he *depicted* in his novel.
Darwin *contributed* to the thinking of his time.
The trial balloon *produced* little understanding of the issue.

PAST PERFECT

Past perfect distinguishes between the times of different actions or conditions in the past. This tense is almost always used with the past:

By the time the host *arrived*, the guests *had departed.* (*arrived*, past; *had departed*, past perfect)
Napoleon *had* already *been defeated* when the news *arrived* that additional supplies *were* available. (*had been defeated*, past perfect; *arrived*, past; *were*, past)
The trees *had lost* their leaves before winter *arrived.* (*had lost*, past perfect; *arrived*, past)

PRESENT PERFECT

Present perfect describes an action or condition begun in the past, but not yet completed:

The tanker *has plowed* the seas for nine months.
John *has permitted* his children complete freedom.
Baseball *has* long *been* a popular sport in America.

Future Tenses

The future tenses are *future* and *future perfect*.

FUTURE

Future describes future actions or conditions:

The ship *will depart* next Wednesday.
Careful preparation *will assure* satisfactory results.
Orwell's world *will* never *be* acceptable to most of us.

FUTURE PERFECT

Future perfect is perhaps the most infrequently used of all tenses. It describes conditions or actions that will occur before another future action and so *normally* appears with the present tense used to describe future actions and *infrequently* with the future tense:

> The basket *will have arrived* before the ship *departs.*
> We *shall have eaten* all we want long before the meal *ends.*
> The publisher *will have exhausted* all copies of the first printing before he *will reprint* the book.

In the first two examples, the future perfect is combined with the present; in the third example, the future perfect is combined with the future. The present and the future can be interchanged in all three sentences.

TENSE	*Past Perfect*	*Past*	*Present Perfect*
	action completed before a previous past action	action completed in the past	action begun in the past that continues in the present
ACTIVE	I had called You had called He had called We had called You had called They had called	I called You called He called We called You called They called	I have called You have called He has called We have called You have called They have called
PASSIVE	I had been called You had been called He had been called We had been called You had been called They had been called	I was called You were called He was called We were called You were called They were called	I have been called You have been called He has been called We have been called You have been called They have been called
PROGRESSIVE ACTIVE	I had been calling You had been calling He had been calling We had been calling You had been calling They had been calling	I was calling You were calling He was calling We were calling You were calling They were calling	I have been calling You have been calling He has been calling We have been calling You have been calling They have been calling
PROGRESSIVE PASSIVE (exists only in *present* and *past)*		I was being called You were being called He was being called We were being called You were being called They were being called	

VOICE

Verbs are in two voices: *active* and *passive*. When a verb is active, the subject performs the action. When a verb is passive, the subject is acted upon.

You surely recall the grammatical order of the sentence—subject, verb, object.

When the *logical subject* of a sentence—the person or thing that would logically be performing the action—is in the *grammatical subject position,* the verb is active. When the *logical object* is in the *grammatical subject position,* the verb is passive.

Consider the following examples:

The manager *fired* his ablest employee.

Present	*Future Perfect*	*Future*
present action, habitual action, simple future	action completed before a future action	simple future action
I call	I will have called	I will call
You call	You will have called	You will call
He calls	He will have called	He will call
We call	We will have called	We will call
You call	You will have called	You will call
They call	They will have called	They will call
I am called	I will have been called	I will be called
You are called	You will have been called	You will be called
He is called	He will have been called	He will be called
We are called	We will have been called	We will be called
You are called	You will have been called	You will be called
They are called	They will have been called	They will be called
I am calling	I will have been calling	I will be calling
You are calling	You will have been calling	You will be calling
He is calling	He will have been calling	He will be calling
We are calling	We will have been calling	We will be calling
You are calling	You will have been calling	You will be calling
They are calling	They will have been calling	They will be calling

I am being called
You are being called
He is being called
We are being called
You are being called
They are being called

Who did the firing? The manager. He is the logical subject and occupies the grammatical subject position. *Fired* is active.

The ablest employee *was fired* by the manager.

Who did the firing? The manager. *Manager* is the logical subject but is placed in the modifier of the verb. The grammatical subject, *employee*, is the logical object; he is the one who was fired. *Was fired* is passive.

Toy boats *are* often *constructed* of polyurethane foam.

The logical subject—the boat manufacturer—does not appear in the sentence. The grammatical subject *boats* is the logical object. The verb *are constructed* is passive.

The boy *left* his briefcase at school.

Who performed the action? The boy. *The boy* is the logical subject and is in the grammatical subject position. *Left* is active.

The man *was fired* and *returned* home disconsolate.

This sentence has two main verbs. The subject of *was fired* is *man*. *Man* received the action. Who fired him? The answer is his boss. *Was fired* is passive. The subject of the second verb, *returned*, is man. Since he is the logical subject as well as the grammatical subject, *returned* is active. Thus we see that sentences may contain both active and passive verbs.

There are four patterns that reveal a passive verb:

1. Some form of the verb *to be* is used with the simple past of the verb, forming the past participle—a verb form used as a modifier.
2. The logical object is in the grammatical subject position.
3. The verb is followed by a modifier that begins with *by*.
4. The logical subject is missing.

The distinction between active and passive is first a matter of definition, a way of classifying verbs grammatically. Of more importance is the effect of these verbs on the vigor of writing style.

In general, vigorous writing relies primarily on active verbs; passive verbs make less vigorous sentences. This is not to say that passive verbs should never be used.

Emphasis is the first consideration in ordering the logical elements of a sentence. Where emphasis demands that a certain word or phrase be given first position in a sentence—the position attracting first attention—put it there. The question of the effect of verbs on style is considered at length in Lesson 9.

REVIEW EXERCISES

Underscore the **verbs** *in the following sentences. Over each verb place A for active or P for passive; identify each tense. Answers to the first ten are on page 102.*

          A fut.   **A pres.**
Sample: I will leave when he returns.

1. After a long wait for a child who could not find his shoes, the family was ready to go.

2. I had hoped for only a few, but there were eleven packages on the platform waiting for delivery.

3. As we were leaving, he bought a double serving of vanilla ice cream.

4. Although he is only five years old, he is known by every person in the neighborhood.

5. All the effort that had gone into the project was wasted.

6. We watched as the boys tripped over fishermen and fishing poles, stepped over boxes of bait, and slapped each other with dead flounders.

7. We shall have destroyed more than fifty empty crates by the time the day has ended.

8. A play on that subject automatically becomes one of the greatest hits of the year.

9. Far more than Dickens, Collins depended upon the technique of the popular sensational theater; how closely is shown by the ease with which he adapted several of his novels to the stage.

10. No one today is so modern as Shakespeare, who owes a little of his freshness to Shaw's mudslinging.

11. The day will soon come when biologists will have solved the mystery of inherited characteristics.

12. Before the long day came to a close, the boys had found all they needed for their report.

13. When a task is brought to successful conclusion, the feeling of good will that prevails is shared by all.

14. We learned that the shad were still running in the Hudson despite the adverse weather conditions that prevailed.

15. They will have to catalogue all the books in the collection before the public is permitted to see them.

16. The East is still suffering from a drought that has lasted for four years.

17. The desk has been lying in the storeroom for eleven months.

18. He has worked on the problem for so long that his reason for undertaking his project is no longer clear.

19. By the time they finish the soup, the meat will be ready.

20. Of all the considerations involved, honesty must prevail.

LESSON 7

Agreement and Reference

AGREEMENT

Agreement is the relationship between a verb and its subject. Singular verbs must have singular subjects; plural verbs must have plural subjects:

> Each student does his own homework.
> Men find work necessary.

In these simple sentences, agreement between subject and verb is obvious. In more complicated sentences, faulty agreement may occur because the writer fails:

1. to identify the correct subject and verb.

> Often a scientist such as Einstein or Newton, or others like them, make a vital contribution to mankind. (The subject is *scientist*, and the verb must be *makes*.)
> Often scientists such as Einstein makes a contribution to mankind. (The subject is *scientists*, and the verb must be *make*.)

2. to recognize that such words as *one, each, either, another, none, neither, someone, somebody,* and *everyone* are singular.

> One of the students are ready with their term paper. (The subject is *one*, and the verb must be *is*. There is another mistake in this sentence—*their* refers to *one* and must be *his*. This mistake is faulty reference, which will be discussed in the next section of this chapter.)
> Another of the students are to attend the concert. (The subject is *another*, and the verb must be *is*.)

39

3. to treat collectives consistently. Collectives are subjects or objects that are singular when they refer to a group, plural when they refer to the members of a group. Once the writer establishes whether a collective is singular or plural, he must be consistent.

> The pastor's congregation were unanimous in approving his proposal. The congregation was silent on the other questions. (The writer used *congregation* as a plural in the first sentence and must retain that plural when he uses it the second time.)

REFERENCE

Reference is the term used for the relationship between a subject or object and a *pronoun*—a word that replaces a subject or object or when repetition would be undesirable:

> A teacher has many responsibilities. He must provide for all the students in his classes. (The pronoun *he* replaces teacher in the second sentence.)
> The American Kennel Club sets the standards for dogs. It requires dog owners to register their dogs at birth. (In the second example there are two pronouns. *It* replaces Kennel Club, and *their* replaces owners.)

Faulty reference can occur when sentences are so complicated that the writer loses track of the word that the pronoun is to replace:

A. One of the properties that belongs exclusively to verbs and verb forms are tense.
B. Maugham takes anyone from a gigolo to a lord and develops them with equal ease and finesse.
C. The next year he had an attack of appendicitis; it broke before he could be rushed to the hospital.

In sentence A the subject *that* of the dependent clause refers to *properties;* since *that* (replacing a plural) is plural, the verb should be *belong.* Since *one* is singular, its verb must be *is.* This sentence contains errors of both reference and agreement.

In B *them* refers to *anyone*. Since *anyone* is singular, the pronoun should be *him*.

In C the problem of reference is different from that in A and B. The pronoun *it* cannot refer to anything in the preceding clause. What really broke was the man's appendix—not mentioned in the sentence.

A similar problem occurs in the following sentence. Can you find the error?

He suffered a measles attack; they kept him in bed two weeks.

CASE

Although the form of an English word does not usually change when the function of the word has been changed, we are familiar with the change needed to show possession. Consider the *boy's* book. The apostrophe and the letter *s* show that the boy owns the book. This form is the possessive case.

There are three cases in English: subjective, possessive, and objective.

Possessive presents little difficulty in English. All the student has to remember is that if the sentence element is singular, he must add apostrophe and *s*. If the sentence element is plural, he must add *s* and apostrophe.

a boy's book (one boy)
boys' books (more than one boy)

Subjective and objective cases present difficulty only when used with pronouns. Consider the word *stone* used as subject, object, or modifier. It remains *stone*.

Pronouns are another matter.

I have a book. (subjective)
My book is here. (possessive)
The book is *mine*. (possessive)
The librarian gave *me* the book. (objective)

I has become *my* and *mine* and *me*.

There are similar pattern changes for *you, he, she, we,* and *they*.

In formal English, the linking verb *to be* is followed by the subjective case: It is I; it is he; it is she.

The possessive of *it* is troublesome. The form is *its*. Remember that *its* is the form corresponding to *his*. Never put an apostrophe in this word to show possession. (*It's* is a contraction of *it is*.)

REVIEW EXERCISES

Some of the following sentences contain errors in agreement or reference. Correct them wherever they occur.

1. Entrepreneurial drive is one of those aspects of human potentiality that is not easily destroyed, and a businessman will be able to do business under even the most adverse circumstances.

2. One of the teachers who specializes in literature gave a talk on Shakespeare to the entire senior class.

3. Perhaps some day each person will have their own helicopter for commuting to work.

4. After satisfactorily completing basic training, almost every soldier is sent to a specialized training school, depending on their particular ability.

5. The faculty was unable to agree on examination policy, and so they adjourned for another week.

6. He decided not to pursue any of the careers suggested by his parents because he doubted that it was suitable for him.

7. There are fourteen men in the department, and everyone of them are important to its future.

8. Either rain or snow are going to fall tomorrow.

9. He was examining the man's head who hoped to qualify for the experiment.

10. He suffered a measles attack. They confined him to the house for the entire month.

11. The flour and ground rice is thoroughly mixed to form the desired dough.

12. She is one of those suburban housewives who thinks that the welfare of the community comes before the welfare of the family.

13. The committee gives their opinion only after hours of deliberation.

14. The Supreme Court, after initially refusing to hear the case, have now decided to hear it.

15. At the top of the legislative agenda are a civil rights bill.

16. The Congressman—and his aide, incidentally—were concerned with the tax legislation.

17. I gave this to whoever could use it.

18. Everybody who dislike the candidate deride his decisions.

19. Unprecedented acclaim is awaiting an architect or city planner who can solve the middle income housing problem.

20. Putting themselves in the place of the pet owner, the legislator realized that they had a valid point.

For answers to the first ten sentences, see page 103.

LESSON 8

Punctuation

Punctuation groups the thoughts within a sentence into units for the convenience of the reader. Writers employ the period, comma, semicolon, colon, dash, question mark, exclamation point, parentheses, quotation marks, and ellipsis to perform this function.

PERIOD, QUESTION MARK, EXCLAMATION POINT

These three marks are used to end a sentence. Since no one has any trouble using them, full discussion is not necessary. For uses of these marks with quotation marks, see page 56.

COMMA

Commas are used to punctuate

- nonessential modifiers
- introductory modifiers
- words or groups of words in series
- two or more independent clauses
- a variety of special uses

Punctuating Nonessential Modifiers

A nonessential modifier is one that is not necessary to identify the unit it modifies. It adds information to an already modified unit.

George Washington led his troops in a number of campaigns.

We know perfectly well who Washington was. Any information we add about him will be nonessential. His name is enough to identify him.

George Washington, *who was to become President of the United States,* led his troops in a number of campaigns.

The clause *who was to become President of the United States* is a nonessential modifier. It must be set off by commas.

Examine these two sentences:

A. My uncle *who lives in Ohio* is an electrician.
B. My uncle, *who lives in Ohio,* is an electrician.

In A, the writer shows that he has more than one uncle by using no commas. The modifier *who lives in Ohio* is essential. Without it, we do not know which uncle is an electrician. In B, the writer has but one uncle, and the modifier *My* identifies him. *Who lives in Ohio* is nonessential, as shown by the use of commas.

Ernest Hemingway, *noted American author,* wrote of the heroic aspects of war.

Heminway's name is enough to identify him. The modifier is nonessential and has to be punctuated.

All Americans who think clearly favor an excellent public education system.

All Americans might seem to be sufficient identification of the subject of the sentence, but it is not. The writer does not mean all Americans, but only those *who think clearly.* This is an essential modifier and must not be punctuated.

He was beloved by a large majority of the staff, *although the public found his manner repulsive.*

The clause *although the public found his manner repulsive* is a nonessential modifier of the main verb *was beloved.* It does not limit or define the original statement, but adds nonessential information. Regardless of what anyone else thought of him—the public, his children, the members of his country club, his automobile dealer—he was beloved by a large majority of the staff.

Flight 703 was delayed for thirty minutes, *though the airline had announced it would arrive on schedule.*

The clause *though the airline had announced it would arrive on schedule* is a nonessential modifier. It does not limit or define anything in the main statement. The fact is that Flight 703 was delayed for thirty minutes. The airline's announcement is not essential, nor would the condition of the pilot and crew, the on-time arrival of most other planes, the state of the weather, or any of a dozen other circumstances be essential to the main statement. Any nonessential modifier added to this sentence would have to be set off by commas.

The plane *delayed thirty minutes by fog* carried several foreign diplomats.

The modifier *delayed thirty minutes by fog* is necessary to identify the plane and must not be punctuated. It is the only identification we have of the plane that carried the diplomats. The flight number was not supplied. We have no other way of knowing what plane the writer had in mind.

He was delayed *because the train did not arrive on time.*

In this sentence, *because the train did not arrive on time* answers the essential question"why?" The clause is therefore essential and must not be punctuated.

Do you recall the other questions we ask of the verb to find its modifiers? When? where? how? how much?

Rewriting the original sentence to answer these questions, we have:

He was delayed *yesterday.*
He was delayed *in St. Louis.*
He was delayed *by the breakdown of an earlier train.*
He was delayed *for three days.*

All of these modifiers are essential and are not punctuated. The fact that they are single words or phrases, rather than clauses, makes it obvious that they must not be punctuated. But even of they could have been expressed in clauses, they would not be punctuated.

Certain nonessential modifiers are inserted in sentences for rhetorical purposes—that is, to heighten the effect of the sentence in some way. All these modifiers—such as *of course, for example, so to speak, to say the least,* and *however*—are set off by commas:

> He was, *however,* one of our main hopes in the game.
> Caesar showed excessive personal ambition, *to say the least.*
> Muriatic acid, *for example,* is used to clean tiles.
> Music soothes the savage beast, *so they say.*

The test of whether to punctuate a modifier involves asking the question: If I omit the modifier, will the word modified still be adequately identified? If the answer is yes, do not punctuate.

Punctuating Introductory Modifiers

An introductory modifier precedes the subject of a sentence but is not joined to that subject. Writers can do no wrong by setting off all introductory modifiers by a comma. There is a tendency, fostered by newspapers and popular magazines, to omit the comma after short introductory phrases that are closely related to the sentence.

The distinction between a closely related modifier and one not closely related is almost always arbitrary. If you have any uncertainty about whether or not to set off introductory modifiers, *set them off.*

The following are examples of sentences containing introductory modifiers that may be interpreted in both ways:

> *In the afternoon* people like to rest.
> *Slowly but surely* he came to an understanding of the subject.
> *During the trial* the defense attorney presented a convincing case.

In the next two sentences, clarity demands that the introductory modifiers be set off by commas:

By afternoon, papers were signed giving the prisoner his reprieve.

By night, trains were able to make their way across the repaired tracks.

Omitting the comma after either of these introductory modifiers might confuse the reader. We surely do not want him to think we are writing of *afternoon papers* or *night trains.* These sentences illustrate the necessity of punctuation to avoid misleading a reader.

Punctuating a Series

A series is three or more grammatical units performing a similar function in a sentence. The series may contain single words, phrases, or clauses. Any sentence element—subject, verb, object, or modifier —may be written in the form of a series.

Punctuating a series is a simple matter: every unit in a typical series must be punctuated.

Consider the following sentences, each of which contains a series made of single words:

Rocks, stones, and boulders fell down the mountainside.

Boys *swim, fish, and play* in summer camps.

The *hot, humid, and crowded* city was more than he bargained for.

Note that a comma was used before *and* in each of these examples to avoid misinterpretation. Note also that no comma follows the final unit in a series unless the series must itself be set off by commas, as in the following sentence:

His catch, which consisted of two flounders, five bluefish, and twelve porgies, made Walton happy.

The series of three has its own internal commas, and a pair of commas encloses the modifying phrase that is the series. Because the modifying phrase is nonessential, it must be set off.

The following sentences contain series composed of phrases or clauses:

> He was certain that his candidate was *aware of the issues, alert to the political dangers of his position, and faithful to his party precepts.*
>
> *At the movies, at the beach, and at the fairgrounds,* thousands of people were finding relief from the heat.
>
> *Afraid that a poor book would harm his reputation, distressed lest the critical reception be unfavorable, and warned by his publisher that another failure would mean loss of his contract,* the author buckled down to a summer of hard work.
>
> A mathematician *who sets up his problem logically, who applies his basic knowledge, and who uses his imagination* seldom fails.

Punctuating Independent Clauses

An independent clause contains a subject and verb and does not depend on any other sentence element for its meaning. Independent clauses are connected by (1) *a semicolon* alone, (2) a semicolon with a *connecting word,* or (3) a *comma* with one of the following common connecting words: *and, but, or, nor, for, so,* and *yet.*

Examine the following sentences:

> The problem that confronted them could be solved in several ways, and John tried all possible solutions.
>
> He decided to walk to town, but he quickly tired.
>
> You can save your money for your old age, or you can enjoy your money in your youth.

When two or more clauses in the same sentence have separate grammatical subjects, a comma is used before any connecting word that introduces an independent clause. In each of the three sentences just given, notice that each independent clause has a separate subject: problem, John; He, he; You, you. A comma must be used before the connecting words.

There are two tests for determining whether clauses are independent:

1. Each clause must have a separate subject.
2. Each clause must be able to stand as a sentence when the connecting word (and, but, or, nor, for, so, yet) and the comma are dropped.

Let us apply test number 2, since all the clauses have separate subjects. The three sentences become:

The problem that confronted them could be solved in several ways. John tried all possible solutions.
He decided to walk to town. He quickly tired.
You can save your money for your old age. You can enjoy your money in your youth.

All three of the sentences have passed tests 1 and 2. They are independent. A comma is needed before the connecting word that joins the independent clauses.

A sentence that has three or more independent clauses is treated as a series. If the clauses are short, they are separated by commas, and the final element is preceded by *and, or,* or *but.* If the clauses are long, they are separated by semicolons, with the exception of the final element, which is set off either by a semicolon or by a comma with the conjunction.

Political conventions have the responsibility of seeking out acceptable candidates; the delegates are aware of this responsibility, and the result is a consensus.

The three clauses are independent because they have different subjects, and each clause can stand as a separate sentence.

Other Uses of the Comma

DATES

A comma sets off the year from the day of the month and from any sentence element that follows:

Bloomsday was June 16, 1904.
June 16, 1904, was Bloomsday.

No comma is used between a month and a year when no date is supplied:

Germany declared war on Russia in August 1914.
August 1914 marked the beginning of World War I.

The military practice of stating the date before the month also eliminates the comma:

10 June 1943

ADDRESSES

A comma sets off a larger geographic unit from a smaller one and from any sentence element that follows:

Many railroad lines terminate in Chicago, Illinois.
The League of Nations had its headquarters in Geneva, Switzerland.
Chicago, Illinois, is the terminus for many railroad lines.
Geneva, Switzerland, was the headquarters of the League of Nations.

DIRECT ADDRESS

Commas set off the expression used in direct address:

Gentlemen, I give you the King!
Hey, are you ready to leave?
If you can, John, meet me at the library.
Try to solve the problem, Harry.

WEAK EXCLAMATIONS

Commas set off weak exclamations—exclamations not strong enough to merit an exclamation point:

Well, I would have gone if you had come along.
Oh, did you really mean what you said?

SEMICOLON

The semicolon is one of the easiest marks of punctuation to use in English. It has two principal uses.

Punctuating Two Independent Clauses

A semicolon separates two independent clauses not linked by a common connecting word (and, but, or, nor, for, so, yet):

> Shakespeare wrote his plays in verse; Oscar Wilde, following a later convention, wrote his in prose.
>
> Men, they say, have been worn out by high office in a few years or even months; Queen Elizabeth I was her own Prime Minister in war and peace for forty years, most of them fraught with danger both to the State and to her own much threatened life.

Semicolons separating clauses are frequently followed by such connecting words as *however, moreover, nevertheless,* and *thus.* In such cases, the connecting word is set off by a comma from the clause that follows it:

> The Royal Dublin Society had expelled Count Plunkett from membership because he was the father of an executed rebel; however, he went to the polls with the backing of a good part of Nationalist Ireland.
>
> Foundations have supplied a great deal of money for research in science; nevertheless, much more money will have to be expended before many basic scientific questions are resolved.

Punctuating Internally Punctuated Series

Semicolons set off elements of an internally punctuated series:

> July 4, 1776; April 6, 1917; and December 7, 1941, are important dates in American history. American homes are generally built of wood, a favorite in the East; masonry, a favorite in large cities; and stone, a favorite in rural communities.

COLON

A colon is primarily used to introduce a formal series or a formal explanation. The sentence element following the colon may be a single word, a phrase, or a clause:

> He admired three Impressionist painters: Matisse, Monet, and Manet.
>
> The technical report contains four important sections: the abstract, a concise statement of the main findings of the study; the introduction, a brief statement of the background of the study; the body, a complete account of all procedures; and the conclusions.
>
> The Continental Army spent the winter at Valley Forge: no other suitable winter quarters could be found.
>
> The automobile's aerodynamic design was outstanding: it enabled the automobile to achieve speeds of two hundred miles an hour.

Introducing Long Quotations

While a comma will suffice before quotation marks that enclose a *short* quotation, a colon is used to introduce a *lengthy* quotation. In the latter case, the quotation itself is not usually enclosed in quotation marks, but is set off from the main text by additional indentation.

Examples:

> Marx and Engels wrote, "The history of all hitherto existing society is the history of class struggles."
>
> When Lady Macbeth dies, Macbeth foresees his own end. He knows what is before him:
>
>> Tomorrow, and tomorrow, and tomorrow
>> Creeps in this petty pace from day to day
>> To the last syllable of recorded time;
>> And all our yesterdays have lighted fools
>> The way to dusty death. Out, out, brief candle!

> Life's but a walking shadow; a poor player
> That struts and frets his hour upon the stage,
> And then is heard no more. It is a tale
> Told by an idiot, full of sound and fury,
> Signifying nothing.

While this example is taken from poetry, a quotation from prose would be handled in the same way:

> In *The Moral Equivalent of War,* William James wrote:

>> Modern war is so expensive that we feel trade to be a better avenue to plunder; but modern man inherits all the innate pugnacity and all the love of glory of his ancestors. Showing war's irrationality and horror is of no effect upon him. The horrors make the fascination. War is the *strong* life; it is life *in extremis;* war-taxes are the only ones men never hesitate to pay, as the budgets of all nations show us.

Colon and Semicolon with Independent Clauses

There sometimes is confusion about whether to use a colon or a semicolon between independent clauses. Use a colon when the second clause deals specifically with some element in the first clause, explaining or justifying the claim of the first clause, as in this sentence:

> The apple tree is deciduous: it sheds its leaves in winter.

Use a semicolon when the second clause is related closely enough to the first to justify linking them:

> The apple tree is deciduous; the pine tree is coniferous.

Never use a colon before a connecting word such as *however, moreover, nevertheless,* or *thus.* The semicolon should be used:

> Many people write for a living; however, few achieve literary fame.

DASH

The dash is used to isolate a sudden change in thought, a summarizing statement, or an explanation from the remainder of a sentence:

Dogs may be man's best friend—I prefer cats.

Books have been known to change a man's life, influence the conduct of political affairs, and spark great social change—books are potent.

Movies—those produced in Hollywood—show life in America to be ideal.

QUOTATION MARKS

Quotation marks are used to indicate verbatim quotations except when the quotations are lengthy. The quotations may be from a text or from speech.

Quotation from Text

Borrowings of less than five lines are enclosed in quotation marks and are incorporated into the text. These quotations are normally preceded by a comma or a colon, as shown on page 53. A comma is used when the quoted material is informal; a colon is used when the material is formal.

> The lecturer said, "All we have to do is keep our heads in the months ahead of us."
>
> Lincoln's Gettysburg Address begins: "Fourscore and seven years ago our fathers brought forth upon this Continent a new nation, conceived in liberty and dedicated to the proposition that all men are created equal."

It is often possible to quote material in a sentence without using any punctuation in addition to quotation marks. This is true when the material quoted is limited to a word or a few words:

> Bagehot characterized the "special laws of inheritance" as unknown.

Quotation from Speech

In punctuating direct quotations from speech, several conventions must be followed:

1. Within the sentence, a comma precedes any direct quote.

John said, "I am going home."

2. If an interpolated remark—a remark inserted in a text—occurs within a direct quote, it must be set off by commas in the following manner:

> "I feel that all is going wrong," John said, "but I will do my best."

Note that the first comma occurs inside the quotation marks, the second outside.

Quotation Marks with Other Marks of Punctuation

There are three conventions concerning marks of punctuation other than quotation marks coming after quoted material:

1. Periods and commas are always placed inside the quotation marks.

2. Colons and semicolons are always placed outside the quotation marks.

3. Question marks and exclamation points are placed inside quotation marks if they are part of the quotation, outside when they are not:

> She asked, "Are you going?"
> She really said, "I have never seen an automobile"!

Quotations Within Quotations

When a quotation occurs within another quotation, the first quotation uses double quotation marks, the second single:

> He said, "Remember that Hippocrates' aphorism, 'Ars longa, vita brevis' applies to all of us."

Generally, when a single quotation and double quotation end together, the single quote comes before the double quote, but *after* the final punctuation mark:

As an eminent critic remarked, "Hemingway exploits the simple declarative sentence, such as 'This man was bareheaded.'"

There are certain cases in which this general rule does not apply. In quoting a question within a quotation, the question mark falls between the single quote and the double quote. No period is needed after the double quote, because the question mark is a terminal mark:

The student asked, "Did Lady Gregory answer the charges made by the critic that she had 'Republican inclinations'?"

The exclamation mark follows the same practice.

Quotation Marks with Words Used in a Special Sense

Words used in a special sense are frequently enclosed in quotation marks:

"Work" has a special meaning in physics.

Students make the mistake of using quotation marks to bolster colloquial or poorly chosen words. Quotation marks will not help. A good word needs no help.

Quotation Marks with Titles

Quotation marks are used with any published work included within another work. Thus, all stories in magazines, all articles collected in books, chapter titles, and poems not separately published are enclosed in quotation marks.

Underline titles of books, magazines, pamphlets, movies, and operas.

GENERAL RULE

A title that appears on the title page of a book should be underlined.

A title that appears elsewhere in a book should be enclosed in quotation marks.

PARENTHESES

Parentheses are used to set off interjected explanatory or qualifying statements within a sentence—or to set off complete statements within a sentence—or to set off complete sentences that are interjected to explain or qualify.

> This special paper (commonly called carbon paper) is used over and over again until it is no longer useful.
> (Macadam is often used in place of more expensive materials for just this reason.)

Note that the period comes inside the final parenthesis when an entire sentence is enclosed. It occurs after the final parenthesis when the parenthetical material comes at the end of a sentence and is only part of the sentence.

ELLIPSIS

Ellipsis is used to indicate the omission of part of a quotation. The mark usually consists of three periods. A fourth period is used when words have been omitted from the end of a sentence.

> Consider Hemingway's analysis of the crowd's behavior: "If the spectators know the matador is capable . . . they will put up with mediocre work . . . . "

The first ellipsis (three periods) indicates that words have been omitted from within the sentence, the second (four periods) the end of the sentence.

REVIEW EXERCISES

Insert punctuation in each of the following sentences where required:

1. The United States Constitution which is a document revered by many has been amended twenty-three times.

2. Before he could find his way three hours had passed.

3. Women have found that they can manage their homes their careers and their hobbies with ease.

4. Shakespeare who wrote more than thirty plays wrote over a hundred sonnets the sonnet form is one of the most frequently used in Elizabethan literature.

5. He thought despite his intuition telling him otherwise that he would try once more to find his cufflinks.

6. July 4, 1776 is an historic date in United States history one every schoolboy must remember.

7. The United Nations of which UNICEF is a part has its headquarters in New York City New York.

8. Gentlemen please

9. Oh I don't care if you do

10. He hoped that she would arrive and that she would bring the package with her.

11. Little can be said for the poem the poet has no ear for the language.

12. There were three kinds of houses in the town houses that were too big houses that were too small and houses that were not houses at all.

13. Books help us spend our leisure hours and so we should be grateful for them.

14. Before dinner on the terrace the couple spent an hour by the pool.

15. Churchill known for his valor Lincoln known for his statesmanship and Washington known for his military leadership surely have lasting places in the history of Western civilization.

16. He was interested in the connotative meanings of words meanings associated or implied.

17. They made several attempts to solve the problem for they could not go ahead without a solution.

18. They sought a solution however all their efforts failed.

19. Two elements made up the chemical solution oxygen and hydrogen sulfide.

20. Melancholy Hamlet cried To be or not to be.

21. Would you rather be rich or happy

22. Don't you think you have had enough peanut butter

23. My youngest uncle who lives in Hoboken has several children.

24. Do not confuse Hoboken New Jersey with Waukegan Illinois

25. People make decisions every day of their lives but too often their decisions are inadequate.

Insert the marks of punctuation needed in the following paragraphs:

Then there is the remarkable case of what is called industrial melanism ＿＿ the fact that during the past hundred years many different species of moths have become black in industrial towns ＿＿ while remaining light and protectively colored in the countryside ＿＿ In these species the melanics ＿＿ are dark forms ＿＿ are much hardier than the normals ＿＿ but these ＿＿ the light ones ＿＿ are better concealed from their enemies in the unblackened countryside ＿＿ So they have a selective advantage there ＿＿ while the melanics are better able to resist the smoke and contamination of the industrial areas ＿＿ Here ＿＿ again ＿＿ the new conditions have nothing whatever to do with the origin of the mutation which results in melanism ＿＿ There were always a few rare melanics ＿＿ much valued ＿＿ incidentally ＿＿ by collectors ＿＿ and the new conditions merely provided them with their opportunity ＿＿

Julian Huxley
Evolution in Action

I went to the woods because I wished to live deliberately to front only the essential facts of life and see if I could not learn what it had to teach and not when I came to die discover that I had not lived. I did not wish to live what was not life living is so dear nor did I wish to practice resignation uless it was quite necessary I wanted to live deep and suck out all the marrow of life to live so sturdily and Spartanlike as to put to rout all that was not life to cut a broad swath and shave close to drive life into a corner and reduce it to its lowest terms and if it proved to be mean why then to get the whole and genuine meanness of it and publish its meanness to the world or if it were sublime to know it by experience and be able to give a true account of it in my next excursion. For most men it appears to me are in a strange uncertainty about it whether it is of the devil or of God and have *somewhat hastily* concluded that it is the chief end of man here to "glorify God and enjoy him forever."

H. D. Thoreau
Walden

There is a class of persons happily not quite so numerous as formerly who think it enough if a person assents undoubtingly to what they think true though he has no knowledge whatever of the grounds of the opinion and could not make a tenable defense of it against the most superficial objections such persons if they can once get their creed taught from authority naturally think that no good and some harm comes of its being allowed to be questioned where their influence prevails they make it nearly impossible for the received opinion to be rejected wisely and considerately though it may still be rejected rashly and ignorantly for to shut out discussion entirely is seldom possible and when it once gets in beliefs not grounded on conviction are apt to give way before the slightest semblance of an argument waiving however this possibility assuming that the true opinion abides in the mind but abides as a prejudice a belief independent of and proof against argument this is not the way in which truth ought to be held by a rational being this is not knowing the truth truth thus held is but one superstition the more accidentally clinging to the words which enunciate a truth.

J.S. Mill
*Of the Liberty
of Thought and Discussion*

For answers to the first ten sentences and the three paragraphs, see pages 104-106.

LESSON 9
Grammar and Style:
Achieving Style Through Grammar

Style in writing means conveying an idea, an image, a thought, a fact, an argument as simply as the complexity of the concept or content permits.

Samuel Taylor Coleridge states: "The infallible test of a blameless style: namely, its untranslatableness in words of the same language, without injury to the meaning." Coleridge meant that the writer who has achieved style has thought through what he wants to say and has so formulated his concept grammatically that it cannot be further reduced without distorting its meaning. Every sentence you write must be examined to satisfy this requirement.

The hallmarks of a good sentence are unity, emphasis, and coherence. *Unity* demands that a sentence have a central idea. Secondary concepts must be subordinated to this central idea. *Emphasis* demands that the important concepts occupy important grammatical positions—subject, verb, and object. *Coherence* demands that the logical relationship of the parts of the statement be clearly discernible to any reader. Thus a good sentence communicates a central concept, places the important parts of that concept in important positions in the sentence, and effectively relates each part of the sentence to every other part.

Here is a sentence that fulfills all these requirements:

A Boston taxicab driver who moved to San Francisco found the everyday speech of his fellows very much like his own.

The discussion concerns a Boston taxicab driver who found the speech patterns in another part of the United States similar to his own. That is the unity of the sentence. The interesting fact that he moved to San Francisco has nothing to do with the sentence unity and is properly subordinated in a modifying clause.

The sentence has proper emphasis because the grammatical subject is also the logical subject, and the verb and object, *found* and *speech,* are also correct logically and grammatically. The criterion of coherence is satisfied because the relationship of the elements of the sentence is clear to the reader.

Now let us see how a poor writer might have structured the same concept:

> A Boston taxicab driver moved to San Francisco and found the everyday speech of his fellows very much like his own.

What has happened to the unity, emphasis, and coherence of the statement? You should know by now that the writer has violated the grammatical principles you have already learned.

The grammatical subject and object have remained the same; however, the sentence has been robbed of emphasis because the verb now is compound: *moved and found.* Instead of focusing on *found,* the reader is now distracted by *moved.* The action of moving is obviously of much less importance than the action of finding. The original sentence properly subordinated the moving by placing it in a modifying clause.

Here is another sentence that meets the requirements of unity, emphasis, and coherence:

> Many of the forms that classical grammarians denounce—for example, the split infinitive, the use of *like* for *as,* and the double negative—are so firmly established in colloquial American speech that any attempt to wipe them out is plainly hopeless.

This sentence has unity, emphasis, and coherence, but can be made more emphatic by three changes:

> Many forms denounced by classical grammarians—for example, the split infinitive, the use of *like* for *as,* and the double negative—are so firmly established in colloquial American speech that any attempt to wipe them out is hopeless.

Do you recognize the grammatical changes that have been made? First, the subject of the original sentence was *many,* which was modified by the phrase *of the forms.* Since we are talking of forms, not many, *forms* has been made the grammatical subject of the rewritten sentence. *Many* is now a modifier. Secondly, the subordinate modifier *that classical grammarians denounce* has been reorganized and shortened to bring *denounced* closer to *forms.* The emphasis placed on *classical grammarians* has been lessened by putting them in a modifying phrase. The result is greater emphasis on the powerful word *denounced.* Finally, *plainly* or any other modifier of *hopeless* is unnecessary. What is more, it detracts from the finality of the judgment.

Now examine a poor sentence. As you read it, keep in mind the hallmarks of unity, emphasis, and coherence:

> There is no disputing that a published and accepted writer in America occupies a unique and often unenviable position as compared with the writer-citizens of other civilized countries.

The subject *there* and the verb *is* perform no useful function. What a waste of two of the three most important grammatical elements in a sentence! Just cutting off the first five words of the sentence would improve it substantially:

> The published and accepted writer in America occupies a unique and often unenviable position as compared with the writer-citizens of other civilized countries.

Since we are talking of the *writers in America,* we have at least put them in the subject position. The verb now is *occupies,* which is what it should be. What further changes can be made to improve this sentence? The latter part of the sentence obviously needs work. There are too many unnecessary modifiers. A better version of the sentence would be:

> The published and accepted American writer occupies a unique and often unenviable position compared with the writers of other countries.

We have gone from twenty-nine words in the original sentence to only twenty in the final form.

EFFECTIVE SENTENCE FORM

While you should strive for excellent sentence form as you make a first draft of anything you write, you will find that editing improves every first draft. As you do that editing, it will be helpful if you bear in mind eight rules for effective sentence form:

- Logical and grammatical subjects must coincide.
- Logical and grammatical verbs must coincide.
- Unimportant concepts must be subordinated.
- Modifiers must be placed as closely as possible to the words modified.
- Modifier length must reflect modifier importance.
- Every modifier must be logically necessary.
- Every word must be from the same general usage level: formal, informal, or colloquial.
- *Every sentence must convey meaning.*

Logical and Grammatical Subjects Must Coincide

When you edit your sentences, the first question to ask is, "What am I discussing?" The answer is the logical subject; it should be put in the grammatical subject position. If it is not there, the reader will have to struggle to find out what you are talking about. The most common faults in regard to subject position result from using *it* and *there* as subjects. They usually have no meaning.

Logical and Grammatical Verbs Must Coincide

When the logical subject is the grammatical subject, ask yourself, "What am I trying to say about the subject?" The answer to that question is the verb. That verb must be as forceful as possible. Avoid excessive use of the verb *to be* in any of its forms. Continual use of this linking verb is a characteristic of poor writers. All they are doing is stating a relationship between a subject and the words that follow. Whenever possible, verbs must state something, not merely link. Excessive use of passive verbs will weigh down your sentences with forms of *to be*. Use of passive verbs places the logical *object* in the grammatical *subject* position, thus emphasizing the object. Use the passive only when you want to emphasize the logical object and de-emphasize the logical subject. For review of active and passive verbs, see Lesson 6.

Unimportant Concepts Must Be Subordinated.

Logically important concepts always occupy grammatically important positions in good sentences. If a logical object exists, it must normally occupy the grammatical object position. Unimportant information must be subordinated: it must be made to modify the important concepts.

Modifiers Must be Placed as Closely as Possible to the Words Modified

Modifiers give precise shadings of meaning to other elements in a sentence. To do their job effectively, they must be placed as closely as possible to the words they modify. Failure to observe this simple grammatical rule obscures or distorts meaning.

Modifier Length Must Reflect Modifier Importance

A modifier can be a single word, a phrase, or a clause. As you increase the number of words in a modifier, you increase the grammatical importance of that modifier. As you edit, ask yourself whether the length of each of your modifiers is justifiable. If it is not, reduce it. If a modifier is a clause, perhaps a phrase will do. If a phrase, perhaps a word. De-emphasizing the importance of a modifier further emphasizes the importance of the central statement.

Every Modifier Must Be Logically Necessary

Unnecessary modifiers kill the words they modify or indicate that the wrong sentence elements were chosen in the first place. The leaves of a tree obscure its structure. Without them, the structure is clearly visible. Thus, unnecessary modifiers always obscure meaning. Pruning them is both a delight and a necessity.

Every Word Must Be from the Same Usage Level

In writing, two things must be considered: the nature of the material and the audience for which it is intended. These two requirements dictate the usage level of the words employed—formal, informal, or colloquial. Once the level of discourse has been established, it must be sustained throughout. Nothing is more incongruous than a mixture of usage levels.

Every Sentence Must Convey Meaning

Everything that has been said up to now should make clear that sentences must convey meaning. We have been concentrating up until now on the individual elements within a sentence, but you must not overlook the complete sentence itself. Successful editing requires that every sentence add meaning to what has gone before. The most fruitful use of the red pencil comes when whole sentences are eliminated. The inevitable result is stronger paragraphs, stronger writing.

This rule should probably have been the first one given, but students and professional writers as well cannot see the emptiness of a sentence until they begin to probe within it. As you search for the logical subject and the logical verb in a sentence in order to make them the grammatical subject and verb, you often find yourself questioning whether the sentence has any logic to it at all.

In the light of what your first sentence says, does your second sentence flow naturally? And your third sentence and your fourth and every other one?

Demanding that every sentence convey meaning leads many times to elimination of whole paragraphs.

REVIEW EXERCISES

Edit the following sentences in the light of the eight rules for effective sentence form. Answers for the first five are on page 106.

1. One session of the United States Congress, which has met each year since the founding of the country in the eighteenth century, is of interest to tourists from all over the United States, including Hawaii and Alaska.

2. Despite all the efforts of the conniving plotters, everything in their scheme to hold up a bank found a way to be something less than a great success.

3. There is very little, if anything, that can be done by doctors who are confronted by a case of old-fashioned measles except sit back in their offices and wait for it to pass.

4. As long as our city believes that crime and murder cannot be overcome, the sociologists will find, much to their dismay, that there is little they can do to make their doctrines as effective as they can become if they were ever given a chance to initiate worthwhile and effective planning.

5. Disbursing public money and public effort with no chance of ever seeing some return for it is the best method of inflaming the voters, which many astute officials have learned to their advantage.

6. The freshman said that he wanted to leave the country in the first paragraph because of oppression of his people, and, in the last paragraph, changed his mind.

7. Judges sometimes punish those prisoners who rebel at the condition of the jails realizing they can't be improved.

8. One of the teachers who remained after school decided, in the interim, to punish their students.

9. My uncle wrote that he would arrive on Tuesday in a telegram.

10. The Internal Revenue Service—the nation's finest—annually persecute many cases of tax evasion.

The Sentence in Context

In the final analysis, sentences are themselves no more than elements within larger units. Just as the grammar of the sentence affects the arrangement of elements within a sentence, there is a grammar of the paragraph that affects the arrangement of the sentences that are its elements. The grammar of the paragraph is less formalized than the grammar we have been discussing all the way through this book, but operates just as effectively.

Where a sentence stands within a paragraph, what its function is, and how it relates to the sentences preceding and following largely dictate its construction. Within a paragraph we generally recognize that individual sentences perform different functions, and these functions place certain constraints upon the sentences. A *topic sentence* introduces the subject of a paragraph; other sentences, which we will call *continuity sentences,* develop the subject; *transitional sentences* connect major elements of the development; *summary sentences* restate and emphasize the subject of the paragraph. Let us examine these types of sentences more closely.

A *topic sentence* tells what the paragraph is about. In most paragraphs it is the first sentence. It normally is composed of two elements, a transitional statement that relates the paragraph to the one that preceded it, and the statement of the hypothesis (point of view) of the paragraph it introduces. The rest of the paragraph supports the hypothesis. The paragraph usually ends when the hypothesis has been adequately supported. However, when a hypothesis requires lengthy proof, it may extend over more than one paragraph. In this case, each paragraph must be clearly structured to show its relationship to the other paragraphs in the line of development. The transitional statement in the topic sentence carries this responsibility.

A *continuity sentence* provides the details that prove the hypothesis stated in the topic sentence. The form of the continuity sentence is determined by the nature of the material and the complexity of the ideas. The major problem in writing continuity sentences is making sure that they all relate to the hypothesis presented in the topic sentence. Failure to do so results in loss of unity, emphasis, and coherence. The reader cannot follow the course of the argument.

A *transitional sentence* supplies the reader with direction either between paragraphs or within a single paragraph when the development of the argument demands an abrupt change in direction. If this need develops often, you are probably writing poor paragraphs. In most writing, a transitional word—relating one thought to another by repetition of a word used in the previous statement—is all that is needed.

A *summary sentence* is sometimes needed at the end of a paragraph to supply emphasis. Generally, the summary statement is an entire paragraph that comes at the close of a paper. Less frequently, it is a sentence or a paragraph coming at the end of one part of a paper. A summary sentence is needed at the close of a paragraph only when the paragraph has presented a particularly important or difficult statement.

The easiest way to appreciate these sentence forms is to examine them in context. The following pages present paragraphs of exposition along with comments on their structure.

PARAGRAPH 1

You cannot have good matter with bad style. Examine the point more closely. A man wishes to convey a fine idea to you. He employs a form of words. That form of words is his style. Having read, you say: "Yes, this idea is fine." The writer has therefore achieved his end. But in what imaginable circumstances can you say: "Yes, this idea is fine, but the style is not fine"? The sole medium of communication between you and the author has been the form of words. The fine idea has reached you. How? In the words, by the words. Hence the fineness must be in the words. You may say, superiorly: "He has expressed himself clumsily, but I can *see* what he means." By what light? By something in the words, in the style. That something is fine. Moreover, if the style is clumsy, are you sure that you can see what he means? You cannot be quite sure. And, at any rate, you cannot see distinctly. The "matter" is what actually reaches you, and it must necessarily be affected by the style.

Arnold Bennett
Literary Taste

COMMENTS ON PARAGRAPH 1

This paragraph illustrates the ability of an author to convey a concept simply and directly. How does Bennett achieve simplicity and directness? By use of:

- present tense
- simple sentences
- one-syllable words
- direct address
- variety of sentence form
- statement of main thought in opening sentence and repetition in closing sentence.

You cannot have good matter with bad style. This topic sentence introduces the hypothesis that the paragraph develops in a dialogue between the author and his reader. A number of short sentences make the argument point by point. The reader's reactions are anticipated by Bennett so he can refute them.

The theme stated in the first sentence appears at first glance to be irrefutable. However, Bennett sees more complications in it and does not wish to have his reader accept the statement without thoroughly understanding what is meant. In order to bring the reader and Bennett to agreement over what the statement means, he starts at a point over which there can be no misunderstanding. He imagines a situation in which a discussion of this topic is taking place. *A man wishes to convey a fine idea to you.* The modifier *fine* rules out of this discussion the problem of *simple* communication. Bennett is obviously talking about communicating subtleties and complexities. The connection between the ideas to be conveyed and the words used to convey them is firmly stated in the next two sentences: *He employs a form of words. That form of words is his style.* We now have a simple definition of *style,* a word first used in the topic sentence. The reader's first reaction is introduced. He has read something and has concluded that it is *fine.* To drive home the point that words are indistinguishable from content, Bennett introduces a situation in which the idea is fine, but the style is thought to be bad. But, according to Bennett, *The sole medium of communication between you and the author has been the form of words.* The fine idea has reached you. *How? In the words, by the words.* Bennett has established that communication can only take place through the medium of words. Since Bennett previously established that words are *style,* he can now restate the hypothesis first introduced in the topic sentence. The *summary sentence*–last in the paragraph–performs this function.

PARAGRAPH 2

The parts of a composition may be poetical, without the composition as a whole being a poem. A single sentence may be considered as a whole, though it may be found in the midst of a series of unassimilated portions; a single word may even be a spark of inextinguishable thought. And thus all the great historians, Herodotus, Plutarch, Livy, were poets; and although the plan of these writers, especially that of Livy, restrained them from developing this faculty in its highest degree, they made copious and ample amends for their subjection, by filling all the interstices of their subjects with living images.

Shelley
A Defence of Poetry

COMMENTS ON PARAGRAPH 2

This paragraph represents an interesting contrast with the illustrative paragraph taken from a work by Arnold Bennett. Shelley's paragraph is composed of only three sentences, each one longer than the preceding one. His final sentence has fifty-two words, while Bennett's longest sentence contains only nineteen. Not only are the sentences longer here, but the words used are more difficult, in contrast with the simple words used by Bennett.

The most striking stylistic characteristic of this paragraph is its plan of development:

- sentence one states the hypothesis
- sentence two develops that hypothesis by making it explicit
- sentence three supplies samples

The topic sentence of the paragraph is the first: *The parts of a composition may be poetical, without the composition as a whole being a poem.* Shelley then refines this generalization by stating that a sentence or even a word may be considered poetical. Finally, to prove this thesis, Shelley cites the work of classical historians.

Shelley assumed his audience to be highly literate. He expected them to be familiar not only with the names, but also with the work, of the historians. The strength of the argument rests on the validity of the examples. The reader's lack of familiarity does not invalidate the argument; it only invalidates the reader. Any reader has the opportunity to verify or negate Shelley's thesis independently. As a consequence, Shelley's argument is stronger than Bennett's. Bennett was writing for a broader and presumably less literate audience than Shelley's. The level of the audience determines to a large extent the selection of words, sentence length, and paragraph construction. This accounts for the stylistic differences between the paragraphs by Bennett and Shelley.

Earlier in this chapter, we stated that a paragraph ends when its hypothesis has been adequately supported. You can see that Bennett and Shelley both followed this precept. How many students do?

PARAGRAPH 3

At least three-fifths of the literature called classic, in all languages, no more lives than the poems and stories that perish monthly in our magazines. It is all printed and reprinted, generation after generation, century after century; but it is not alive; it is as dead as the people who wrote it and read it, and to whom it meant something, perhaps; with whom it was a fashion, a caprice, a passing taste. A superstitious piety preserves it and pretends that it has aesthetic qualities which can delight or edify; but nobody really enjoys it, except as a reflection of the past moods and humors of the race, or as a revelation of the author's character; otherwise it is trash, and often very filthy trash, which the present trash generally is not.

William Dean Howells
Criticism and Fiction

COMMENTS ON PARAGRAPH 3

This stylistically ornate paragraph has only three sentences. The elaborate punctuation serves to break it up into manageable units. The paragraph contains five semicolons and twelve commas.

What is the argument of the paragraph? Most classical literature is trash

What is the proof for this thesis? None.

What, then, is the nature of the paragraph? Howells becomes subjective and emotional when he should be objective and rational.

Howells' target is the segment of classical literature that does not appeal to Howells. He condemns it and the public that supports it. The key to Howells' puritanical attitude is found in the last sentence, in which he characterizes his target as *very filthy trash.* This is a clue to the subjective basis for the entire paragraph.

The most interesting aspect of the paragraph is the grammatical use Howells makes of the underlying metaphoric structure—the pattern of life and death. Much of the diction in the paragraph employs words associated with life and death: *lives, perish, generation, alive, dead, preserves, past.*

Compounds such as *printed and reprinted, generation after generation, century after century, wrote it and read it,* and the series *a fashion, a caprice, a passing taste* are other positive stylistic aspects of the paragraph—even though all elements of the series mean the same thing. The repetition of *trash* in the last sentence is also good.

However, Howells does not define the term *classic,* nor does he tell us which *three-fifths of the literature called classic* he is talking about.

The progression through the three sentences of the paragraph from a relatively short sentence to a longer one and finally to one containing fifty-nine words is an effective way to build to a climax. But the logical failure detracts from the style.

PARAGRAPH 4

A foolish consistency is the hobgoblin of little minds, adored by little statesmen and philosophers and divines. With consistency a great soul has simply nothing to do. He may as well concern himself with his shadow on the wall. Speak what you think now in hard words again, though it contradict every thing you said today—"Ah, so you shall be sure to be misunderstood." Is it so bad then to be misunderstood? Pythagoras was misunderstood, and Socrates, and Jesus, and Luther, and Copernicus, and Galileo, and Newton, and every pure and wise spirit that ever took flesh. To be great is to be misunderstood.

Emerson
Self-Reliance

COMMENTS ON PARAGRAPH 4

This famous paragraph, so typical of Emerson and so beloved by us all, exploits a number of stylistic and grammatical devices:

- variety of sentence length
- dialogue (direct address)
- rhetorical question
- inverted sentence order
- deliberate grammatical patterns for stylistic effect

By now you should be able to identify all the elements listed, with the possible exception of the last. The first deliberate grammatical pattern for stylistic effect is in the second sentence, where the modifying phrase *with consistency* has been consciously moved from its normal position at the end of the sentence. In the next-to-last sentence, instead of using a compound subject composed of all the persons misunderstood, Emerson has Pythagoras as the simple subject, trails all the rest for emphasis, and then summarizes their characteristics in *every pure and wise spirit that ever took flesh*. The conscious retention of the word *and* before each element in that series must also be noted. The final stylistic device is the last sentence—pithy and forceful.

Emerson's paragraph appears, on first reading, to be a logical development of the argument stated in the first sentence. Close inspection reveals faulty paragraph structure. This fault reflects faulty logic that invalidates the hypothesis, which is finally stated in the last sentence.

The paragraph breaks into two parts: great souls are inconsistent; great souls are misunderstood. While Emerson argues logically that to be inconsistent is to be misunderstood, he never proves that misunderstanding results from the inconsistency. Pythagoras, Socrates, Jesus, Luther, Copernicus, Galileo, and Newton surely were misunderstood, but Emerson does not show that the misunderstanding resulted from their inconsistency. We might make our own judgment that this misunderstanding derived from the absolute consistency of their individual beliefs!

Although the opening sentence appears to be the topic sentence, the last sentence is the only one broad enough to include all the statements made in the paragraph. To prove this, we will reverse the order of the sentences in the paragraph, changing only the italicized pronouns to maintain coherence. Notice that in doing this we have shifted the emphasis:

> To be great is to be misunderstood. Pythagoras was misunderstood, and Socrates, and Jesus, and Luther, and Copernicus, and Galileo, and Newton, and every pure and wise spirit that ever took flesh. Is it so bad to be misunderstood? Speak what you think now in hard words again, though it contradict every thing you said today—"Ah, so you shall be sure to be misunderstood." *You* may as well concern *yourself* with *your* shadow on the wall. With consistency a great soul has simply nothing to do. A foolish consistency is the hobgoblin of little minds, adored by little statesmen and philosophers and divines.

You might try turning one of your own paragraphs around in this way when you are having trouble with a particular thought you are trying to describe on paper.

PARAGRAPH 5

A perfect tragedy should, as we have seen, be arranged not on the simple but on the complex play. It should, moreover, imitate actions which excite pity and fear, this being the distinctive mark of tragic imitation. It follows plainly, in the first place, that the change of fortune presented must not be the spectacle of a virtuous man brought from prosperity to adversity: for this moves neither pity nor fear; it merely shocks us. Nor, again, that of a bad man passing from adversity to prosperity: for nothing can be more alien to the spirit of Tragedy; it possesses no single tragic quality; it neither satisfies the moral sense, nor calls forth pity or fear. Nor, again, should the downfall of the utter villain be exhibited. A plot of this kind would, doubtless, satisfy the moral sense, but it would inspire neither pity nor fear; for pity is aroused by unmerited misfortune, fear by the misfortune of a man like ourselves. Such an event, therefore, will be neither pitiful nor terrible. There remains, then, the character between these two extremes—that of a man who is not eminently good and just, yet whose misfortune is brought about not by vice or depravity, but by some error or frailty. He must be one who is highly renowned and prosperous—a personage like Oedipus, Thyestes, or other illustrious men of such families.

Aristotle
Poetics

COMMENTS ON PARAGRAPH 5

This well-known Aristotelian definition (in translation) sets forth four criteria by which a tragedy may be evaluated. The first two sentences, taken together, constitute the topic sentence of the paragraph. Although this construction is unusual, it is not rare. Grammatically, this construction presents a problem. The writer must reunite two sentences that might have been one. The word *moreover* in the second sentence performs this function.

Aristotle's paragraph is unusually well organized. The two sentences which are the topic statement introduce the concept to be developed. The remainder of the paragraph is noteworthy from our point of view for its use of three stylistic devices:

- repetition and reversal of terms
- parallel punctuation and construction
- use of connectives

The words *pity* and *fear* occur throughout the paragraph. Clearly Aristotle used this repetition in order to draw attention to these important aspects of tragedy.

Paired terms are common in the paragraph: *pity and fear, prosperity and adversity, pitiful nor terrible, vice or depravity, renowned and prosperous* are some of them. When a pair is used more than once, Aristotle changes the connecting word or the order of the terms. Consider these two sentences:

> It follows plainly, in the first place, that the change of fortune presented must not be the spectacle of a virtuous man brought from prosperity to adversity: for this moves neither pity nor fear; it merely shocks us. Nor, again, that of a man passing from adversity to prosperity: for nothing can be more alien to the spirit of Tragedy; it possesses no single tragic quality; it neither satisfies the moral sense, nor calls forth pity or fear.

The repetition and reversal of these terms emphasize the important concepts Aristotle is presenting.

Notice further that the translator uses parallel punctuation in these two sentences. Each sentence contains a colon followed by a semicolon. The colon in both sentences is followed by *for,* the semicolon by *it.* In the final two sentences, a dash is used to set off a fuller explanation of a previous concept. The reader surely can find his way with these signposts.

The use of too many connectives such as *as we have seen, moreover, it follows, in the first place, again, doubtless, therefore,* and *then* is a sign of poor writing. Prose cluttered with them masks rather than clarifies the principal ideas. The strength of Aristotle's ideas would have been better served if all the connectives were omitted. You might take your pen in hand to do a little editing of Aristotle's paragraph, eliminating every connective you find. Don't be afraid. Editing is never sacrilegious—particularly when the hand of a translator has already left its mark on a piece of writing.

PARAGRAPH 6

Whatever be the social state a man finds himself in, he may be free. For certainly a man is free, in so far as he is led by reason. Now reason . . . is always on the side of peace, which cannot be attained unless the general laws of the state be respected. Therefore, the more a man is led by reason—in other words, the more he is free, the more constantly will he respect the laws of his country and obey the commands of the sovereign power to which he is subject.

Spinoza
Tractatus Theologicopoliticus

COMMENTS ON PARAGRAPH 6

This translation from the work of Spinoza illustrates the development of a philosophic argument in language any student can understand. The discussion proceeds through the use of a common argumentative device—the syllogism. A syllogism consists of two premises and a conclusion. If the premises are true, the conclusion must be true: if A is B and C is A, then C must be B. Perhaps the most famous syllogism of all time is: All men are mortal. Socrates is a man. Therefore Socrates is mortal. No one can deny the truth of the two premises, the first two statements. The conclusion must therefore be true.

The syllogism involved in the paragraph from Spinoza may be stated as follows: Man has the possibility of being free. Freedom is intertwined with reason. Therefore the more reasonable a man is, the more free he is. Spinoza carries his argument one step further, equating freedom with respect for social and political institutions.

The form of any syllogism demands repetition of terms in the premises and the conclusion. In the paragraph from Spinoza, the word *free* is repeated, and the word *reason* is repeated. Purposeful repetition of words improves emphasis.

Another word repeated for emphasis is *more*. In the last sentence, it appears three times: "the *more* a man is led by reason—in other words, the *more* he is free, the *more* constantly will he respect the laws of his country .... " In order to throw emphasis on the final *more*, the translator has shifted *will* from its normal position and placed it before the subject *he*.

He convinces us of the validity of his argument through grammar:

- repetition of words in the syllogism
- repetition of a word for emphasis
- shifts in normal grammatical patterns to emphasize words not normally emphasized

PARAGRAPH 7

The leaves of the water plantain, all from the root, are olive green, strongly veined, and elliptical but very variable in shape, broader or longer, and sometimes heart-shaped at the base. The flower-stem is tall and symmetrically branched, displaying the three-petaled, very small white or rarely delicate pink flowers to great advantage. The flowers are perfect, with six stamens and a pistil; they are possibly self-fertilized, but more probably cross-fertilized by the beelike droneflies, all pollen-eaters and honey-drinkers. The plant is one to three feet high, and is found in the shallow water of ponds and sluggish streams everywhere.

*Grass: The Yearbook
of Agriculture/1948*

COMMENTS ON PARAGRAPH 7

This paragraph is intended to enable the reader to identify the water plantain when he comes upon it. It must, therefore, be clearly expressed in terms the reader will understand. The paragraph names the colors of each of the plant parts.

The paragraph is not logically constructed. There are four sentences: the first describes the leaves of the plant; the second, the flower stem and the flowers; the third, the structure of the flowers and the means of pollination; the last the entire plant and its habitat.

Expositional sentences logically proceed from the general to the particular, or from the whole to the parts. Variation of this basic paragraph structure should be employed consciously to achieve a desired stylistic effect. In this case, the paragraph structure appears to be accidental. The simplest way to repair the paragraph is to make the last sentence the first one and continue on through the rest of the sentences as they now appear.

A striking aspect of this paragraph is its reliance on the verb *to be*. While this verb is not strong, it is characteristically found in paragraphs of description. Replacing this verb by an active verb may lead to incongruity in an expository work such as a handbook of wild flowers. How would you like to read *The plant stands one to three feet high* instead of *The plant is one to three feet high?* When you consider that every description in the handbook states the height of the plant, you must agree that *stand* would become more offensive than *is*.

We cannot leave this paragraph without commenting on its excessive hyphenation. Styles of punctuation change, as do styles of spelling and styles of dress. Would you hyphenate (1) heart-shaped, (2) flower-stem, (3) three-petaled, (4) self-fertilized, (5) cross-fertilized, (6) drone-flies, (7) pollen-eaters, and (8) honey-drinkers?

PARAGRAPH 8

In view of the state of knowledge concerning livestock husbandry and the scarcity of labor, the first colonists turned their livestock loose on the unoccupied lands adjacent to their holdings as a matter of course and depended on the natural vegetation to carry them at all seasons. The realization that the rigorous winters of the more northern latitudes dictated shelters and supplies of fodder came slowly. As a system of mixed farming prevailed in all the earliest settlements, the protection of growing crops from the depredations of livestock was a prime necessity. Enclosures or fences of some kind were obviously needed, but fencing would have taken more labor than could be spared from clearing land, providing shelter, and cultivating crops. Out of this situation emerged forms of range husbandry which, generally speaking, were repeated again and again during the course of the American westward movement.

Grass: The Yearbook
of Agriculture/1948

COMMENTS ON PARAGRAPH 8

This paragraph introduces the topic of range husbandry, developed in succeeding paragraphs. The first four sentences are a unit; all deal with the reasons for the emergence of open ranging in the Colonies. The fifth sentence introduces a new concept, that various forms of range husbandry emerged with the westward expansion of the United States. The discussion of these forms is left to the paragraphs that follow.

The paragraph structure is dictated by the purpose the paragraph serves—to introduce a topic for discussion. In such an introductory or transitional paragraph, the subject to be discussed subsequently must be presented close to the end of the paragraph.

The Yearbook of Agriculture is a United States Government publication, distributed to thousands of readers across the country. Since the audience for this writing is a cross-section of Americans, how suitable is the style?

The opening sentence begins with a phrase that contains unnecessary complications. *In view of the state of knowledge concerning* applies to *the scarcity of labor* as well as to *livestock husbandry.* Logically, the two phrases have no connection. In the main statement, the phrase *as a matter of course* is unnecessary. Finally, the pronoun *them* is too far removed from the word it refers to.

In the second sentence, the subject *realization* and the verb *came* are too far apart. At first glance, the reader thinks that *the realization* or *winters of the more northern latitudes dictated shelters and supplies of fodder.* (Clearly, *dictated* is incorrect for the concept involved. *Required* would be a better choice.) The sentence should read, "The realization came slowly that the rigorous winters of the more northern latitudes required shelters and supplies of fodder."

The diction of the third sentence is elaborate. *Depredations* is surely not the word the writer had in mind. Regardless of the word substituted for *depredations,* the writer should have brought his subject and verb, *protection . . . was,* closer together than he did.

The last two sentences are satisfactory.

All expository writing for a broad audience should be characterized by clarity rather than by stylistic elegance. This paragraph suffers because the attempt at stylistic elegance detracts from the clarity.

PARAGRAPH 9

Old age comes to trees, as to all other living organisms. The span of life of a tree is specific. Gray birch is old at 40. The sugar maple lives longer, up to 500 years. Some oaks may live 1,500 years, junipers 2,000 years. Some of the giant sequoias are believed to be about 4,000 years old. Old trees are like old people—the infirmities of age are upon them. They have difficulty with respiration (its rate in old plants is much lower than in young plants); the annual shoots are not so vigorous as they once were; and the weakening cambium activity is reflected in the formation of fewer and fewer wood cells. Hence, the annual rings become narrower. As the rate of growth of the tree decreases, dead branches appear in ever-increasing numbers. The recuperative capacity of an old tree is impaired, and its wounds do not heal over so easily as before. The leaves become smaller; their moisture content decreases; the tree finds it more and more difficult to provide water for its vital functions; the inflow of food to the growing points drops; and the growth hormones probably cannot be transported in large enough quantity to the places where they are needed.

Trees: The Yearbook
of Agriculture/1949

COMMENTS ON PARAGRAPH 9

This paragraph brings to life a subject that many people consider dry. How does it achieve this effect?

Suppose you were given a subject like this to write about. Would you have enough imagination to begin by associating trees with all other living organisms—by inference with man himself? *Old age comes to trees, as to all other living organisms.* The reader is immediately involved in the exposition.

From this beginning, the paragraph develops two concepts. First, the age of trees is discussed, beginning with the birch, which has the shortest life span, and extending to the patriarch, the sequoia. The transition to the second concept occurs when the author returns to his original analogy, using the word *old* again to tie his second concept in with the topic sentence: *Old trees are like old people—the infirmities of age are upon them.* From that point on, the paragraph gives the specific maladies that attack old trees.

Specific sentences in the paragraph are worthy of note. The one beginning *They have difficulty with respiration* summarizes the three main difficulties faced by old trees. Yet the author wishes to comment on the first of these difficulties. If he does so in another sentence, he will have to give undue emphasis to a relatively unimportant concept and he will interrupt his line of development. He chooses to insert a parenthetic comment *(its rate in old plants is much lower than in young plants)* in the midst of listing all the infirmities. A parenthetic statement is traditionally used when material alien to a line of development needs insertion. This device is effective only when used sparingly. Frequent insertion of parenthetic material makes the reader feel that the writer did not spend enough time organizing his material before he began to write.

The last sentence in the paragraph describes the effects of old age on trees. As the series progresses, the tree is closer and closer to death. The cycle is contained within a single sentence—a series of five clauses separated by semicolons. The unity of the thought is thus sustained.

PARAGRAPH 10

There is no flavor comparable, I will contend, to that of the crisp, tawny, well-watched, not over-roasted, *crackling,* as it is well called—the very teeth are invited to their share of the pleasure at this banquet in overcoming the coy, brittle resistance—with the adhesive oleaginous—O call it not fat—but an indefinable sweetness growing up to it—the tender blossoming of fat—fat cropped in the bud—taken in the shoot—in the first innocence—the cream and quintessence of the child-pig's yet pure food: the lean, not lean, but kind of animal manna—or, rather, fat and lean (it must be so) blended and running into each other, that both together make but one ambrosian result, or common substance.

Lamb
Dissertation upon Roast Pig

No Comment.

Final Test

*Underscore the subject and verb of each **independent** clause in the following sentences:*

1. Despite all the efforts of the police force, the crime rate in the city continued to rise.

2. We are bound to find that they are satisfied with our work if we have worked as hard as we possibly can.

3. The committee found that its meetings of the past six months yielded no tangible results, because insufficient thought had been given to the most pressing problem of all.

4. Little is known about the customs of the indigenous population, and no one seems willing to devote the time needed to produce the required information.

5. No apparent motive can be found for the crime; the investigation will be dropped.

6. All through the night, the men kept at their shovels, but not until the bulldozer arrived was there any chance of finding the loot.

*Underscore the subject and verb in each **dependent** clause of the following sentences:*

7. As long as we were able to find our way, the darkness did not keep us from our journey.

8. A good fire in a friendly fireplace has long been known as a comfort, suitable company for an evening with a good book.

9. The method that he found most practical proved to be the one that he followed from then on.

10. The interior decorator decided that his client needed to make her own decisions.

11. I felt sorry that there was little left to do because the project had held my interest for so long.

The italicized modifiers in each of the following sentences relate to a principal sentence element. Write S *(subject),* V *(verb), or* O *(object) over each modifier to indicate its relationship to one of the sentence elements:*

12. *As long as the game lasted,* John watched *carefully*.

13. English, *the only subject in the curriculum that the boy enjoyed,* was taught *badly*.

14. *Much modern* art finds *its* adherents *among those who admire experimentation for its own sake.*

15. *Even when Daniel Boone was well past eighty,* he moved *farther* west *to escape intruders when he discovered that a family was building a cabin only ten miles away.*

16. *In the early years of the depression, many* Americans found themselves *in great financial difficulty.*

17. *If the truth be known,* recommendations *for employment* are *often* made *on a scientifically unacceptable basis.*

Underscore all verbs in the following sentences:

18. Despite all the advantages that came to him because of his father's wealth, the young man was unable to find his way in life.

19. Integral calculus is often made a requirement for first-year college students.

20. Although the major part of the structure was incomplete, the people of the town showed great pride in their achievement.

21. Similarities between the behavior of farm animals and undomesticated animals make it difficult for us to dismiss the role of heredity in forming behavior patterns.

22. The gentlemen took their coffee in the dining room, while the ladies adjourned to the parlor.

23. Finally the discussion came to an end, and the members began to leave, feeling that they had spent the evening well: the entertainment and the enlightenment gained had been even greater than expected.

Fill the blanks in the following sentences with the appropriate forms of the verbs indicated in parentheses:

24. Once the evening service is over, we (go)   home to eat.

25. The sailors decided that they (take)   shore leave if the ship arrived on time.

26. The director tried to have his actors portray the emotions the playwright (intend)

27. I usually (coordinate)   two sentences if I (be) able to do so.

28. He has worked at his job for ten years, but he (find) himself unable to continue.

29. When I arrived, he   already (leave)

Correct all errors in agreement and reference in the following sentences.

30. Among his problems is complete lack of interest in his work and loss of ambition.

31. We have ruled out the condition of the grandfather's property since they have no relevance.

32. Leslie Howard gave one of the memorable performances of Hamlet; the critic described his performance as sensitive and moving.

33. The fact that some things are associated with other things in time do not mean that a causal relationship exists.

34. I gradually forget the rules of punctuation as I read through book after book, but I must reacquaint myself with it when I begin to write.

35. One of the most effective devices for recording music directly from the radio are now for sale.

36. Every one of the thousands of students who apply for admission to college find that they are eventually admitted somewhere.

Supply the necessary punctuation in the following paragraph:

37–50. The substantial changes in Great Britain's economy the social and political changes that followed them and the vigorous discussion of different concepts of government provided a new setting for British party politics in the nineteenth century. During the closing years of the Napoleonic Wars two features of the political system were well established the influence of the monarch was in sharp decline and the Tory Party was dominant in Parliament. George III spent the last nine years of his life in complete insanity. At his death in 1820 his eldest son who had served as regent succeeded him as George IV and reigned for ten years. He was a gross headstrong man who quickly ruined his political influence when himself a notorious sinner he sought a divorce from his wife in the opening months of the reign. The scene of the trial was the House of Lords and the proceedings there as well as the comings and goings of George and his wife Caroline in the streets of London attracted general attention and grew into a national scandal. The King failed to gain a divorce however he succeeded in barring Caroline from the coronation ceremony. The King acted against the advice of his ministers throughout the rest of his reign.

For answers, see page 107.

Answers

INITIAL TEST

Count two points for each correct sentence. Total possible, 100.

1. Although they had done all they could, the <u>engineers</u> <u>failed</u> to complete the project on time.

2. Scholarly <u>work</u> often <u>leads</u> to practical results, even if the scholars have no thought of practicality when they begin to work.

3. The two <u>brothers</u> <u>decided</u> that there was not enough work to keep them busy.

4. The <u>space</u> initially occupied by the Center <u>is</u> modest by graduate school standards; the total <u>area</u> <u>is</u> twelve thousand square feet.

5. <u>New York City</u> <u>has</u> long <u>been known</u> as the center of education in the United States, but <u>many</u> <u>have criticized</u> New York for its numerous innovations in pedagogy.

6. The <u>novels</u> of Joyce Cary <u>have reached</u> thousands of readers, and his posthumous <u>fame</u> <u>has exceeded</u> that which he enjoyed in his lifetime.

7. When <u>they</u> <u>arrived</u> at the beach, the boys quickly stripped to their underwear.

8. John turned out to be an excellent host and showed concern for everyone at the party.

9. The business <u>that</u> <u>was</u> for sale did not suit any of the prospective purchasers.

10. All of us hoped that <u>nothing</u> <u>would be done</u>.

11. I was amazed by his interest since <u>he</u> <u>had</u> always <u>avoided</u> me in the past.

12. *As he wa͜lked along the street,* McCann daydreamed.

13. Macbeth, *Shakespeare's only stru͜cturally uncomplicated play,* is one *o͜f his shorter tragedies.*

14. William Butler Yeats is *the mo͜st widely admired, by*

v   s

common reader and sophisticate alike, of all modern poets who have

written in English.

                o

15. He explained *his unusual and complex* product.

    v   s

16. *In 1854,* the life of Israel Potter, *an historical writer,* was

               v

serialized *in a popular magazine.*

              v

17. *If he abided by the decision,* he would find himself *at a*

          v

considerable disadvantage.

18. The lackadaisical student <u>plodded</u> through his work dispiritedly and finally <u>dozed</u>.

19. History <u>is studied</u> by those who <u>seek</u> insight into today's political problems.

20. When <u>built</u>, the Center <u>will be operated</u> by the United States Public Health <u>Service</u> and <u>will study</u> a broad range of environmental health problems.

21. The educational gap between the average rural child in America entering school and the average urban child <u>is</u> enormous, educators <u>are saying</u> aloud for the first time.

22. He <u>said</u> hello and almost <u>smiled</u>.

23. We <u>began</u> to chat in a friendly manner, and he <u>said</u> that these people <u>had</u> to be taught how to live, how to clean house, and how to look after children.

24. After the evening newspapers appeared, I looked for the review of the play that had opened last night.

25. I looked to see whether he was joking.

26. Each morning, as the sun rises (<u>or</u> rose), the milkman sets (<u>or</u> set) out on his rounds.

27. Before the ship had left, they delivered the flowers.

28. The most important fact the police know about him is that he worked in the bank for ten years.

29. The longest home run ever hit in Yankee Stadium was hit by Babe Ruth.

                                               is

30. The form of your bibliography and footnotes <u>are</u> not standard.

31. A novel or a biography <u>are</u> equally acceptable as the subject of the paper.
(is)

32. Modern research concentrates on those types of disease that <u>affects</u> the greatest number of people.
(affect)

33. This group of essays is concerned with the problems of American democracy.

34. The text of *Moby-Dick* with editorial notes <u>make</u> a fine addition to his personal collection.
(makes)

35. The tweed jacket, bought long ago from one of London's best tailors, serves as his sports jacket even today.

36. J. Dover Wilson, one of the few Shakespearean critics who <u>senses</u> the importance of the passage, realizes that a large part of the Elizabethan audience would have followed the technicalities of the duel in Hamlet as intently as a modern audience follows a poker game in the movies.
(sense)

37—50. Intelligence and creativity are not identical, but intelligence does play a role in scientific creativity—a role greater than it plays in some other forms of creativity. One may summarize by saying that the minimum intelligence required for creative production in science is considerably better than average, but that given this, other variables contribute more to variance in performance. It must also be noted that special abilities—numerical, spatial, verbal, and so on—play somewhat different roles in different scientific fields, but that ability must in no case be below average. A cultural anthropologist, for example, has little need for great facility with numbers. An experimental physicist, on the other hand, does require facility with numbers, although he need not have great facility with words.

LESSON 1: REVIEW EXERCISES

Score 10 for each correct sentence. Total possible, 100.

1. The fat girl ate the food.
   S   V   O

2. Newspaper reporters and editors clarify the news.
   S   S   V   O

3. The lake shone and sparkled.
   S   V   V

4. The call came last night.
   S   V

      S   V   O   O   O
5. Last night he called his mother, sister, and brother.

        S   V   IO   O
6. The veterinarian gave the horse an examination.

    S   V   O
7. The cat mothered her kittens.

    S   V   O
8. Frogs make pleasant sounds.

    S   V   O
9. Honey attracts bees.

     S   V
10. Nothing remained.

LESSON 2: REVIEW EXERCISES

Score 10 for each correct sentence. Total possible, 100.

  S V   S   V
1. I work harder in one day [than most people work all week].

  S V   V   O   S   V
2. [If I *had* not *lost* my car keys], I *would have driven* to work.

     S   V   O   S V   O
3. [Although this was my first speech], I was not nervous at all.

         S   V   O
4. [Because this tree was the finest example of its type in the
                    S   V
country], agricultural agents, from far and wide, came to see it.

        S   V   O
5. Some writers follow all the conventions of standard English;
S   V   O   S   V
others seem to do all [they can to avoid this practice]. (*that* is

understood before *they*)

        S   S   V   V
6. Students [who are not prepared for complicated questions]
V   O
usually get poor grades.

         S   S   V   O   O   V   O
7. Some chairs [that have arms and backrests] are comfort-
S   V   O
able; others, lacking them, are also comfortable.

          S   V   O
8. Successful businessmen show concern for the welfare of
            V   S   S   V   O
their employees, and there is little doubt [that they owe much of
their success to this concern].

       S   S   V   O

9. Schoolteachers [who never permit colloquial expressions in

                          V   O

their students' writing] might be considered old-fashioned; however,

  S   S V   S   V

laxness in writing by students [who feel] [that they can get away

                     V

with anything] cannot be admired.

                 S   V

10. Quotation marks are used for titles of written works shorter than volume length, for single poems, short stories, and magazine articles.

LESSON 3: REVIEW EXERCISES

Score 10 for each correct sentence. Total possible, 100.

        MV   MS   S   V MIO IO   MO   O

1. Generally, old houses give their owners much trouble.

      MS   MS   S   V   MO   O   MV

2. The long-winded orator wound his way [through the tortuous speech].

               MS   MS S   V MO O

3. [Running through the room], the boy stubbed his toe.

      MS   S   MV   V   MO   O   MV

4. Many physicians now caution their patients [against smoking].

      MS   S   V   MV   MV

5. Apple trees blossom vigorously [in the spring].

      MS   MS   S   V   MV

6. [Defeated in battle], the army retreated [to the fort].

     S   V   MV

7. Little can be done [after a show has closed].

      MS S   MS   S   V   MO   MO   O

8. The sea and the wind buffeted the struggling ship, [which

MO

was far off course].

      MS   S   V   MV   MV   V   MO   MO

9. The boy tried hard and finally mastered the difficult

O

subject.

        MV   MS   S   V   O   MO   O

10. [Far off to his left], the gladiator saw lions and other beasts

MO

[coming at him].

LESSON 4: REVIEW EXERCISES

Score one for each element marked correctly. Total possible, 100.

```
      MS    S   V MO   MO    O         MV        S      V
   Correct diction is the basic element [in writing]. Words have to
V   MV    V              S          V           O           MS
be well chosen], [for precision increases clarity and interest]. Good
   S       V   MO    O                    MO
diction means the absence [of ambiguity, obscurity, and misunder-

standing].
      MS     S                 MS              V       MO
   General words, [unlike some scientific ones], have [more than
      O             MO     O       MS   S   V  MV
one] meaning and [more than one] quality. Most words do not
MV         V                 MV                    S     MV
simply denote (the meaning found in the dictionary); they also
     V     S    V     O                      MO
connote—they imply meanings [in addition to the denoted mean-
      MS    S    V    MO     O              MO         O
ing]. Many words have similar denotations, but different connota-
                S    V   MO    O          MO           S
tions; for example, we have many words [meaning dog].   You
     V    O     MO    MO  MO          MO   S V   MO    O
consider these: canine, cur, mongrel, and mutt. It is quite obvious
                              MO
[that mutt, although it means a kind of dog, connotes much more to
                                                    S      V
the reader than simply a dog of undetermined lineage]. Canine is
      MO       O          MO        O              MO
[much more] formal and [also much less] visual [than mutt—it is
               MS     S                MS
less connotative]. The situation [in which we would choose one of
                       V                    MV
these words for dog] would be determined [by the degree of
                       S    V   MO     O          MO
formality in a paper]. Words have different degrees [of appropriate-
                          S            MS
ness to different writing situations]. Writers [who wish to use words
      V    MO      O                   MO
precisely] have the responsibility [of considering all aspects of a

word].
                       MS                   MS   MS    S     MV
   [In addition to all his problems of style], the good writer must
V    MO    O                          IO
pay careful attention [to denotation and connotation as he works].
   MS   S     V    MO    MO     O
Good writing demands this careful attention.
```

LESSON 5: REVIEW EXERCISES

Score 10 for each correct sentence. Total possible, 100.

1. Allen Tate was born in Kentucky and was graduated from Vanderbilt University.

2. That is no country for old men.

3. They sat together at a table that was close against the wall near the door of the cafe and looked at the terrace where the tables were all empty except where the old man sat in the shadows of the leaves of the tree that moved slightly in the wind.

4. Using quotation marks to call attention to an ironic or humorous passage is like poking someone in the ribs when you have reached the point of a joke.

5. Since the days of the early Greeks, men have been trying to explain various natural phenomena and find the laws governing them.

6. The Declaration, then, makes sense, and excellent sense.

7. It has been said that if a person were to take a cup of water to the Pacific Ocean, pour it in, and then stir the ocean thoroughly, he would have eight or ten of the original molecules in the cup if he filled it again with ocean water.

8. A man may take to drink because he feels himself a failure, and then fail all the more because he drinks.

9. Modern English is full of bad habits which spread by imitation and which can be avoided if one is willing to take the necessary trouble.

10. The texts are concerned with political ideas.

LESSON 6: REVIEW EXERCISES

Score 10 for each correct sentence. Total possible, 100.

1. After a long wait for a child who could not find his shoes, the family was ready to go.

2. I <u>had hoped</u> [A past perfect] for only a few, but there <u>were</u> [A past] eleven packages

on the platform waiting for delivery.

3. As we <u>were leaving</u> [A past prog.], he <u>bought</u> [A past] a double serving of vanilla ice

cream.

4. Although he <u>is</u> [A pres.] only five years old, he <u>is known</u> [P pres.] by every

person in the neighborhood.

5. All the effort that <u>had gone</u> [A past perf.] into the project <u>was wasted</u> [P past].

6. We <u>watched</u> [A past] as the boys <u>tripped</u> [A past] over fishermen and fishing

poles, <u>stepped</u> [A past] over boxes of bait, and <u>slapped</u> [A past] each other with dead

flounders.

7. We <u>shall have destroyed</u> [A future perf.] more than fifty empty crates by the

time the day <u>has ended</u> [A pres. perf.].

8. A play on that subject automatically <u>becomes</u> [A pres.] one of the

greatest hits of the year.

9. Far more than Dickens, Collins <u>depended</u> [A past] upon the tech-

nique of the popular sensational theater; how closely <u>is shown</u> [P pres.] by

the ease with which he <u>adapted</u> [A past] several of his novels to the stage.

10. No one today <u>is</u> [A pres.] so modern as Shakespeare, who <u>owes</u> [A pres.] a little

of his freshness to Shaw's mudslinging.

LESSON 7: REVIEW EXERCISES

Score 10 for each corrected sentence. Total possible, 100.

1. Entrepreneurial drive is one of those aspects of human

potentiality that <u>is</u> [are] not easily destroyed, and a businessman will be
able to do business under even the most adverse circumstances.

2. One of the teachers who specializes in literature gave a talk
on Shakespeare to the entire senior class.

3. Perhaps some day each person will have their own helicopter
for commuting to work.

4. After satisfactorily completing basic training, almost every
soldier is sent to a specialized training school, depending on their
particular ability.

5. The faculty was unable to agree on examination policy, and
so they adjourned for another week.

6. He decided not to pursue any of the careers suggested by his
parents because he doubted that it was suitable for him.

7. There are fourteen men in the department, and everyone of
them are important to its future.

8. Either rain or snow are going to fall tomorrow.

9. He was examining the man's head who hoped to qualify for
the experiment.

10. He suffered a measles attack. They confined him to the
house for the entire month.

LESSON 8: REVIEW EXERCISES

Score 10 for each correct sentence. Total possible, 100.

1. The United States Constitution, which is a document
revered by many, has been amended twenty-three times.

2. Before he could find his way, three hours had passed.

3. Women have found that they can manage their homes, their
careers, and their hobbies with ease.

4. Shakespeare, who wrote more than thirty plays, wrote over
a hundred sonnets: the sonnet form is one of the most frequently
used in Elizabethan literature.

5. He thought, despite his intuition telling him otherwise, that
he would try once more to find his cufflinks.

6. July 4, 1776, is an historic date in United States history,
one every schoolboy must remember.

7. The United Nations, of which UNICEF is a part, has its headquarters in New York City, New York.

8. Gentlemen, please!

9. Oh, I don't care if you do.

10. He hoped that she would arrive and that she would bring the package with her.

(These paragraphs are not scored.)

Then there is the remarkable case of what is called industrial melanism—the fact that during the past hundred years many different species of moths have become black in industrial towns, while remaining light and protectively colored in the countryside. In these species the melanics, or dark forms, are much hardier than the normals, but these—the light ones—are better concealed from their enemies in the unblackened countryside. So they have a selective advantage there, while the melanics are better able to resist the smoke and contamination of the industrial areas. Here, again, the new conditions have nothing whatever to do with the origin of the mutation which results in melanism. There were always a few rare melanics—much valued, incidentally, by collectors—and the new conditions merely provided them with their opportunity.

Julian Huxley
Evolution in Action

I went to the woods because I wished to live deliberately, to front only the essential facts of life, and see if I could not learn what it had to teach, and not, when I came to die, discover that I had not lived. I did not wish to live what was not life, living is so dear; nor did I wish to practice resignation, unless it was quite necessary. I wanted to live deep and suck out all the marrow of life, to live so sturdily and Spartanlike as to put to rout all that was not life, to cut a broad swath and shave close, to drive life into a corner and reduce it to its lowest terms, and if it proved to be mean, why then to get the whole and genuine meanness of it, and publish its meanness to the world; or if it were sublime, to know it by experience, and be able to give a true account of it in my next excursion. For most men, it appears to me, are in a strange uncertainty about it, whether it is of the devil or of God, and have *somewhat hastily* concluded that it is the chief end of man here to "glorify God and enjoy him forever."

H.D. Thoreau
Walden

There is a class of persons (happily not quite so numerous as formerly) who think it enough if a person assents undoubtingly to what they think true, though he has no knowledge whatever of the grounds of the opinion, and could not make a tenable defense of it against the most superficial objections. Such persons, if they can once get their creed taught from authority, naturally think that no good, and some harm, comes of its being allowed to be questioned. Where their influence prevails, they make it nearly impossible for the received opinion to be rejected wisely and considerately, though it may still be rejected rashly and ignorantly, for to shut out discussion entirely is seldom possible, and when it once gets in, beliefs not grounded on conviction are apt to give way before the slightest semblance of an argument. Waiving, however, this possibility— assuming that the true opinion abides in the mind, but abides as a prejudice, a belief independent of, and proof against, argument—this is not the way in which truth ought to be held by a rational being. This is not knowing the truth. Truth, thus held, is but one superstition the more, accidentally clinging to the words which enunciate a truth.

J.S. Mill
*Of the Liberty
of Thought and Discussion*

LESSON 9: REVIEW EXERCISES

Judge your own performance. While there are many ways to correct the errors in these sentences, your corrected version should correspond closely with the corrected sentences below.

1. There are two thoughts here that should not be combined in one sentence. Either write as two sentences, or delete the incongruous material in the original sentence: (a) Congress has met every year since the founding of the country. Tourists from all over the United States have always enjoyed visiting Congress. (b) American tourists have always enjoyed visiting Congress.

2. The crooks failed to hold up the bank.

3. Doctors, confronted with a case of old-fashioned measles, can only wait for it to pass.

4. As long as our city believes that crime cannot be overcome, sociologists will be unable to make their doctrines effective.

5. Many astute politicians have learned not to irritate voters by needlessly disbursing public money.

FINAL TEST

Count two points for each correct sentence. Total possible, 100.

1. Despite all the efforts of the police force, the crime <u>rate in</u> the city <u>continued</u> to rise.

2. <u>We are bound</u> to find that they are satisfied with our work if we have <u>worked</u> as hard as we possibly can.

3. The <u>committee</u> <u>found</u> that its meetings of the past six months <u>yielded</u> no tangible results, because insufficient thought had been given to the most pressing problem of all.

4. <u>Little</u> <u>is known</u> about the customs of the indigenous population, and <u>no one seems</u> willing to devote the time needed to produce the required information.

5. No apparent <u>motive</u> <u>can be found</u> for the crime; the <u>investigation</u> <u>will be dropped</u>.

6. All through the night, the <u>men kept</u> at their shovels, but not until the bulldozer arrived <u>was</u> there any <u>chance</u> of finding the loot.

7. As long as <u>we were</u> able to find our way, the darkness did not keep us from our journey.

8. A good fire in a friendly fireplace has long been known as a comfort, suitable company for an evening with a good book.

9. The method that <u>he found</u> most practical proved to be the one that <u>he followed</u> from then on.

10. The interior decorator decided that his <u>client</u> <u>needed</u> to make her own decisions.

11. I felt sorry that there <u>was</u> <u>little left</u> to do because the <u>project</u> <u>had held</u> my interest for so long.

12. As long as the <u>game lasted</u>, <u>John</u> ^vwatched ^v<u>carefully</u>.

13. English, <u>the only subject in the curriculum</u> that the boy^s <u>enjoyed</u>, was taught <u>badly</u>.^v

14. Much <u>modern</u>^s art finds <u>its</u>^o adherents <u>among those who</u> admire <u>experimentation</u> for its own sake.^s ^v

15. Even when Daniel <u>Boone was</u> well past eighty, he moved^o ^v farther west <u>to escape intruders</u> <u>when he discovered that a family</u> <u>was building a cabin only ten miles away</u>.

16. In the early years of the depression, many Americans found
themselves in great financial difficulty.

17. If the truth be known, recommendations for employment
are often made on a scientifically unacceptable basis.

18. Despite all the advantages that came to him because of his
father's wealth, the young man was unable to find his way in life.

19. Integral calculus is often made a requirement for first-year
college students.

20. Although the major part of the structure was incomplete,
the people of the town showed great pride in their achievement.

21. Similarities between the behavior of farm animals and
undomesticated animals make it difficult for us to dismiss the role of
heredity in forming behavior patterns.

22. The gentlemen took their coffee in the dining room, while
the ladies adjourned to the parlor.

23. Finally the discussion came to an end, and the members
began to leave, feeling that they had spent the evening well: the
entertainment and the enlightenment gained had been even greater
than expected.

*(In sentences 24-29, where two acceptable answers are given, the
first is the formal, the second the informal.)*

24. Once the evening service is over, we will go home to eat.

25. The sailors decided that they would take shore leave if the
ship arrived on time.

26. The director tried to have his actors portray the emotions
the playwright had intended (intended).

27. I usually coordinate two sentences if I am able to do so.

28. He has worked at his job for ten years, but he finds himself
unable to continue.

29. When I arrived, he had already left.

30. Among his problems is complete lack of interest in his work
and loss of ambition.

31. We have ruled out the condition of the grandfather's
property since they have no relevance.

32. Leslie Howard gave one of the memorable performances of
Hamlet; the critic described his performance as sensitive and moving.

33. The fact that some things are associated with other things in
     does
time do not mean that a causal relationship exists.

34. I gradually forgot the rules of punctuation as I read through
                                   them
book after book, but I must reacquaint myself with it when I begin
to write.

35. One of the most effective devices for recording music
                      is
directly from the radio are now for sale.

36. Every one of the thousands of students who apply for
                        finds   **he**   **is**
admission to college find that they are eventually admitted
somewhere.

37–50. The substantial changes in Great Britain's economy, the
social and political changes that followed them, and the vigorous
discussion of different concepts of government provided a new
setting for British party politics in the nineteenth century. During
the closing years of the Napoleonic Wars, two features of the
political system were well established: the influence of the monarch
was in sharp decline and the Tory party was dominant in Parliament.
George III spent the last nine years of his life in complete insanity.
At his death in 1820, his eldest son, who had served as regent,
succeeded him as George IV and reigned for ten years. He was a
gross, headstrong man who quickly ruined his political influence
when, himself a notorious sinner, he sought a divorce from his wife
in the opening months of the reign. The scene of the trial was the
House of Lords, and the proceedings there, as well as the comings
and goings of George and his wife Caroline in the streets of London,
attracted general attention and grew into a national scandal. The
King failed to gain a divorce; however, he succeeded in barring
Caroline from the coronation ceremony. The King acted against the
advice of his ministers throughout the rest of his reign.

Index

Eugene Ehrlich and **Daniel Murphy** are co-authors of *The Art of Technical Writing, Writing and Researching Term Papers and Reports,* and *College Developmental Reading.*

Eugene Ehrlich is a member of the Department of English and Comparative Literature, School of General Studies, Columbia University. He also serves as a consultant to industry in the improvement of written and spoken language.

Daniel Murphy teaches at the Baruch College, City University of New York, and was for many years supervisor of the Reference Collection of the New York Public Library. He has been a Guggenheim Fellow and is a specialist in modern Irish literature.

Catalog

If you are interested in a list of fine Paperback
books, covering a wide range of subjects
and interests, send your name and address,
requesting your free catalog, to:

McGraw-Hill Paperbacks
1221 Avenue of Americas
New York, N.Y. 10020